SELLING REAL ESTATE SERVICES

SELLING REAL ESTATE SERVICES

THIRD-LEVEL SECRETS OF TOP PRODUCERS

ROBERT A. POTTER

WILEY

John Wiley & Sons, Inc.

Published by John Wiley & Sons, Inc., Hoboken, New Jersey
Published simultaneously in Canada

For general information on our other products and services or for technical support, please contact our Customer Care Department within the United States at (800) 762-2974, outside the United States at (317) 572-3993 or fax (317) 572-4002.

Wiley also publishes its books in a variety of electronic formats. Some content that appears in print may not be available in electronic books. For more information about Wiley products, visit our web site at www.wiley.com.

Library of Congress Cataloging-in-Publication Data:

Potter, Robert A., 1955-
   Selling real estate services : third level secrets of top producers / Robert A. Potter.
   p. cm.
   Includes bibliographical references.
   ISBN 978-0-470-37596-9 (cloth)
   1. Real estate business–Handbooks, manuals, etc.   I. Title.
HD1375.P667 2008
333.33068'8–dc22

                                                                  2008016814

Printed in the United States of America.

10   9   8   7   6   5   4   3   2   1

To Amy, Mike, and Matt: Everything I do is for and because of you.
To my clients and students: Thank you for teaching me.
To my friends and colleagues: Thank you for your input and support.

Contents

PART I   It's About Winning: Why You?   1

Airbag versus Differentiator   2

Chapter 1   Third-Level Selling   5

Vendor Differentiation versus Client Differentiation   5
Level 1: Vendors Pitch (Airbags)   10
Level 2: Preferred Providers Position Their Offering
    Against the Competition's   13
Third-Level Selling: Strategic Partners Differentiate
    on the Client   14
Deliberate Practice: Are Great Sales People Born
    or Made?   16
Deliberate Practice for Third-Level Selling   19

Chapter 2   How (and Why) Clients Choose You   21

How Clients Choose You   22
Client Differentiators   24
Vendor Differentiators   25
Standard Life Investments Real Estate (SLIRE)
    Example   28
Pick Your Battles   33
Deliberate Practice: How (and Why) Clients
    Choose You   35

Chapter 3   Navigating From Vendor (Level 1) to Preferred
    Provider (Level 2)   37

Search Phase: Level 1 - Pitch to Get Invited!   37
Screening Phase: Level 2 - Position versus
    Competition   39
Position Difference, Preference, and Proof   43

Harvesting Specific Testimonials 47
Rank as Proof 48
Experience Is Simply the Name We Give Our
    Mistakes. (Oscar Wilde) 49
Best Outcome 50
Congratulations! You Made the Short List
    of Preferred Providers 53
Deliberate Practice: From Vendor to
    Preferred Provider 56

PART II   **Third Level: From Preferred Provider
    to Chosen Partner**   **59**
Client Eyes 59
Deliberate Practice: Third-Level Client Profile 64

Chapter 4   Accelerating Personal Relationships 67
Find Common Ground to Accelerate
    Relationships 71
The Relationship Game: Three to Five Questions
    to Uncover "Amazing Stories" 71
Deliberate Practice for Accelerating Relationships 78

Chapter 5   Accelerating Professional Relationships 79
"We Research the Hell Out of Them" 80
Raise the Flashlight 81
What's Changed? The Ultimate Strategic Question 83
Looking for CID 84
Give-and-Take Questions 86
Gaining Agreement to Explore Solutions 87
Deliberate Practice to Accelerate Professional
    Relationships 89

Chapter 6   Finding Project/Property Difference 91
"Our Brokers Need to Know our Buildings Better
    Than We Do." 95
"Because You Didn't Ask" 96
Start the Project before the Mandate 97
Deliberate Practice: Project/Property
    Differentiation 99

Chapter 7   Finding and Aligning to Client Preferences   101
            Previous Experience   102
            Educating Client Concerns   103
            What Could Go Wrong?   105
            Client Visions   106
            Your Competition   107
            Unhooking an Incumbant Competitors   109
            Deliberate Practice: Finding Differences in
               Client Preferences   111

Chapter 8   Finding and Aligning to the Client's Decision
               Process   113
            Deliberate Practice: Find and Align to the
               Decision Process   118

Chapter 9   Third-Level Proposals and Presentations   119
            From Vendor-centric to Client-centric   119
            Third-Level Presentations Are Client-centric   120
            Deliberate Practice: Third-Level Proposals and
               Presentations   128

Chapter 10 Pricing and Third-Level Negotiation   131
            We Lost on Price?   132
            "Who Would You Choose If Prices Were The Same?"   133
            Third-Level Negotiating   134
            Deliberate Practice: Pricing and Third-Level
               Negotiation   140

PART III   **Winning without Competition**   **141**

Chapter 11 Third-Level Client Satisfaction   143
            Highly Satisfied (versus Satisfied) Clients
               Twice as Loyal   143
            Take Care of It (Satisfied) and Take Care of Me
               (Highly Satisfied)   146
            Referral: The Best Measure   149
            Client Advocates: Taking Care of You   150
            Deliberate Practice: Delighting Clients   151

Chapter 12   Winning in the Invisible Market   153
     Invisible Market Danger: Unqualified Clients   155
     Does This Client Have the Problems You Solve?   159
     Finding and Aligning to the Service Decision   161
     Deliberate Practice: Winning in the
         Invisible Market   166

Chapter 13   Managing Third-Level Selling Skills   169
     Track Performance Metrics to Drive Third-Level
         Best Practices   170
     Coaching Results Not Just Behavior   173
     Call Preparation and Momentum
         Recommendations   177
     Call Review and Diagnostics   178
     Coaching   179
     Presentations and Recommendations   180

Chapter 14   Final Thoughts   181
     Get with Clients   183
     Enlightened Self-Interest   184

Appendix 1:   *BCCI Value Proposition*   187

Appendix 2:   *Company Message Acceleration Example*   191

Appendix 3:   *Client Profile*   195

Appendix 4:   *Client Profile with Questions*   197

About the Author   199

Index   201

SELLING REAL ESTATE SERVICES

PART I

It's About Winning: Why You?

Congratulations! You made the short list of preferred real estate service providers. The client has decided to design, build, buy, sell, lease, manage, furnish, or finance a property. Now they need to choose the one service provider who will help them get the best outcome with the least risk, effort, time, and fewest surprises. Why should they choose you?

Most sales books and sales training programs teach you how to sell your product or service, but not how to compete and win in the real estate services arena. They teach you how to ask questions, uncover needs, and then position your product or service as a solution. But what happens when the client has already decided to use the products or services that you and your competitors sell, and they are just deciding which service provider to use? They are no longer deciding to use your service. They are simply asking, "Why should I choose you over your best competitor?"

Let's say you are among three competitors selected to present your case in person and answer the client's one remaining question: Why you? Whoever answers that question best in the eyes of the client wins. The others lose. How much do you get paid if you finish second in competition?

So what is the single most important advantage that you would like to communicate as to why this client should choose you over your best competitor?

Is it your experience, your people, or is it your process? Is it the way you listen, customize solutions, or add value? Now ask yourself if any of your competitors can say something that the client perceives as similar. If so, then your offer is what I refer to as an "airbag," an important but undifferentiated offer. Let me explain.

AIRBAG VERSUS DIFFERENTIATOR

If a car salesman enthusiastically told you to buy his car because it had airbags, would you buy it? Certainly not based on that information alone. It is not that airbags are not important. You probably would not buy a car without airbags, but you would not base your choice on something that everybody offers (see Figure PI.1).

"They all say the same thing..."

Airbags: "...more experienced, bigger, knowledgeable, committed, have more offices, more people, work harder, try harder, listen better, customize our solutions, expertise, international platform, put our customers first, create value, know the market better, faster, better, a total solution provider, blah, blah, blah, blah, blah..."

Figure PI.1 Are You Pitching Airbags?

You may be surprised to discover that you, too, are pitching airbags, which is making it more difficult for clients to choose you. Most of the words that you use to sell your services are very similar to words your competitors use. It is not that your airbag message about your experience and capabilities is not important. The client would not have invited you to compete without those capabilities. It's just that those words don't help the client choose you because they don't differentiate you from your competitors. You may believe that you are better, but how does the client know that if you can't communicate it.

If you don't know or can't explain how you are different and better, then clients will be less inclined to:

- See you,
- Listen to your pitch,
- Share their problems,
- Value your services,
- Choose you over competition,
- Pay you what you are worth, or
- Recommend you to others.

Do you have a compelling value proposition? The lack of a clear and compelling preference value proposition is the single biggest source of career dissatisfaction. It makes your job more difficult and threatens your success.

As real estate markets mature and competition increases, the perceived differences between you and your best competitors decrease. You are probably feeling increasingly commoditized as clients begin to view you and your competitors as pretty much the same. Your win rate may be decreasing. More decisions are being made on price, and competitors are "buying" the business

Non Differentiated Offer

If you cannot clearly communicate your value, prospective clients will be less inclined to:

- Meet & Listen
- Share & Explore
- Agree & Commit
- Choose you
- Pay you
- Recommend you

Figure PI.2 Nondifferentiated Offer.

with low-ball bids. But you also may be the victim of your own loss of identity because your message has not evolved with your client's increased choice.

But winning goes well beyond a rational message. As the competition advances into its final stages, it's more the emotional differentiators—trust, confidence, commitment, and passion—that drive choice among finalists.

The objective of Third-Level Selling is to help you find value in the minds of your clients and then align and communicate a client-centric value proposition in order to make it easier for them to choose you.

We will do that by showing how and why clients choose among alternatives and how elite commercial real estate providers build preference and partnership. The bottom line is that you will win and retain more clients.

Chapter 1

Third-Level Selling

When buying your real estate services, do prospective clients view you as a vendor, a preferred provider, or a strategic partner?

Vendors pitch their capabilities. Preferred providers position against competition. Third-Level providers build a partnership with clients.

Elite real estate service providers, the top 5 percent, have the biggest and most profitable clients. They rarely compete on price, and they do well in good and bad markets. What do these elite providers do differently than the rest of us to win new clients and retain the ones they have?

The short answer is that they engage clients at a deeper personal and professional level, a Third-Level that leads to greater success and career satisfaction and less price competition. In this book we will identify and then show you how to master the attitudes and communication skills these elite providers employ to build strategic partnerships, win new business, and retain committed clients.

VENDOR DIFFERENTIATION VERSUS CLIENT DIFFERENTIATION

From the client's perspective, top competitors pretty much look the same. On the other hand, clients feel that their situation, project, property, people, preferences, and process are unique.

Most professionals who sell real estate services are wasting time trying to force clients to recognize and value increasingly nuanced differences in their capabilities (I call this "vendor differentiation.") Elite, Third-Level service providers create client preference by finding and aligning to what is unique about the client, the project, client preferences, and process (I call this "client differentiation.")

Once clients narrow their options to a short list of highly capable alternatives, nuanced differences in capabilities cease to be a factor in their final choice. At this level everybody is qualified. Instead, clients want to work with someone they know and trust, someone who knows *their* industry, *their* market, *their* company, *their* situation, *their* property, *their* preferences, and *their* process better. In other words, instead of wanting to know more about you, they want *you* to know more about them. They don't want to work with a vendor. They want to work with a strategic partner. If you can find and align to that uniqueness, the client will view you as a strategic partner and not just another vendor.

A Tale of Three Landscape Architects

I can demonstrate Third-Level Selling on a small scale with a personal experience. My wife and I decided to remodel our backyard. We had lived in our house in Marin County near San Francisco for 16 years. When we moved there, our first child was two years old, and we initially designed the yard for little children. Now with an 18-year-old and a 13-year-old, we had clearly outgrown the yard.

We wanted a yard that had a pool, a grill area, a sport court, and lots of room for my wife's roses. We were advised to use the services of a landscape architect because otherwise, we were told, there was a risk we would lower the value of our property if we didn't do it right.

Figure 1.1 Old Backyard.

Figure 1.2 Then, Son Mike, Age 2 with Mom, Amy.

Figure 1.3 My Son, Mike Now.

Since I did not know any landscape architects, we did what most clients do. We got referrals from friends and invited a short list of three top professionals to meet with us. The way these three service providers competed for our business illustrates the major themes in Third-Level Selling. See if you can identify the approach that most closely resembles yours.

The Vendor-Pitched Capabilities

When the first provider came over, we sat at the kitchen table where we looked through his brochure and asked him questions. He showed us some great pictures, gave us some good ideas, and made us feel he was well qualified. Unfortunately, he was also very expensive, which caused us to rethink the whole venture, but we continued.

The Preferred Provider Positioned Against Competition

The next day the second landscape architect came by. Once again we sat at the kitchen table to review her brochure. There were great pictures, good ideas, and solid qualifications. She told us how she was different and better than her competitors. She said her clients liked the way she managed the process and that her way of working would mean less work for my wife and me. She also showed us a chart that indicated that she did more projects than anyone in our area, and she provided some nice testimonial letters.

I preferred her over the first vendor because she could potentially reduce my workload and because she had done more work in our area. However, I could not tell if she was really better than the first guy or just better at presenting her capabilities. But at least now we had two capable providers, which would give me some price or service leverage. If her price were similar to the first architect's price I reasoned, then I would choose her.

The Third-Level Provider Established a Partnership by Differentiating on Us

Instead of sitting at the kitchen table, the third landscape architect asked if we could walk around the backyard. While doing so, he asked how long we had lived in the house, where we came from, how many kids we had, what ages, boys or girls, what sports they played, how my wife and I liked to entertain, how the neighbors felt about outdoor music, and whether there would be little children in the yard.

He asked how we liked the large willow tree that covered the yard, and did we know how much its leaves and roots would impact the pool. He told us that he was able to look up our property at the county office before coming over. He said we had a drainage easement that would require a 10-foot setback, which would change the preferred location of the pool.

When we told him there would occasionally be little children in the yard, he suggested putting an automatic cover on the pool for safety. That would also dictate the shape of the pool.

He asked us about budget and time frame. He continued this for about 45 minutes. We then worked together to draft a rough plan of the yard, and he gave us a range of prices and alternatives.

Whom do you think we chose?

Interestingly, the last provider never showed us a brochure. Nor did he discuss his capabilities. He didn't have to. We could tell by his questions that he was quite capable. He spent all of his time finding out about and then aligning to what was unique about us. That gave us a sense of commitment and trust, the emotional differentiators. Without even realizing it, this professional was modeling Third-Level Selling.

Whether you're a broker, lender, designer, builder, or property manager, differentiating on the client is the key to winning in competition. Instead of trying to show a client what is different about you, identify and align to what is different about your client and then watch your competition wither away.

As an aside, I am frequently asked if my backyard parable is a true story. As the say in the movies, it was based upon a true story. We did proceed with the project (see Figures 1.4 and 1.5).

Figure 1.4 Goodbye Old Backyard.

Figure 1.5 Hello New Backyard.

LEVEL 1: VENDORS PITCH (AIRBAGS)

The vast majority of real estate service providers I observe compete with a selling style that I characterize as Level I - The Pitch. A pitch is a vendor-centric statement of capabilities: "I am a broker, a lender, an architect, a manager, and so on." If the client does not have an alternative provider, your vendor-centric pitch will win the business.

But in most cases the client does have a choice—lots of them. That choice lets the client get more selective. In fact, the more choices the client has, the less difference there is between the winner and the first loser.

When clients have choices, they are no longer asking if you can do it. Now they are asking if you can do it better. Your pitch tells the client that you can do it, but it doesn't explain why or how you can do it better. If you can't clearly and succinctly communicate how you are different and better, how does the client choose you?

The Vendor-centric Assumption

Vendors make the very reasonable assumption that their value is in their capabilities and in their experience. Further, if you are vendor-centric, you believe that the more the potential client knows about you, the vendor, the more likely the client will choose you. Don't you feel that way? I know I did.

If you are a vendor, you do most of the talking in client meetings because your objective is to impress with your capabilities and expertise. In your calls, proposals, and presentations, you tell the client who you are, what you do, how you do it, for whom you have done it, and so on. Sound familiar? If so, you are not alone. Eighty percent of the sales calls, presentations, and proposals I witness are vendor-centric pitches.

Early in our careers we are vendor-centric because we are learning the business. For example, commercial real estate brokers will typically go through a three- to seven-year apprenticeship before they branch out on their own. During their apprenticeship, they will learn the basic brokerage capabilities: how to structure a lease, how to value cash flows, or how to create a marketing brochure. In other words they learn how to cook the meal that someone else hunted. After years of executing the business, it is no wonder that we assume that our value is in our capabilities. However, once we become the hunters, strong capabilities are no longer enough to win.

The truth is that your capabilities get you invited to the competition, but they don't win the business unless there are no competitors. At the end of a competitive decision process the only thing that matters is that the client perceives that you will take better care of them than your best competitors would. How do they acquire that perception? Not with more information about you.

LEVEL 2: PREFERRED PROVIDERS POSITION THEIR OFFERING AGAINST THE COMPETITION'S

When the client has a choice, they want to know which service provider is better. Think about a property owner looking for a third-party manager. If there is only one property manager, the choice is obvious. On the other hand, if the client has five property managers from which to choose, how does that client pick the winner?

The choice is made even more difficult when the property managers competing for the business use similar language (Airbags) to describe their services: "We are experienced. We customize our services. We have been in the business for 25 years. We have offices in more places, etc." If the client can't see a difference among alternatives, is it any wonder that that they choose based on the one difference they can clearly see—price? But price is almost always a self-inflicted wound.

Your inability to clearly see or articulate why you are different and better than competitors makes winning critical business that much harder. When a client has choice, they want you to answer three simple questions:

1. How are you different?
2. Why should I prefer that difference?
3. Why should I believe you?

In Chapter 3 we will show you how to accelerate your positioning message by communicating your Difference, Preference, and Proof. That will help you progress from vendor (Level 1) to preferred provider (Level 2).

THIRD-LEVEL SELLING: STRATEGIC PARTNERS DIFFERENTIATE ON THE CLIENT

Pitching your capabilities gets you invited. Positioning those capabilities effectively against competition gets you to the "short list" of preferred providers, but that still is not enough to win the business.

In fact choosing a service provider among quality alternatives is a complex process with many factors or differentiators that influence client preference. As we will explore further in Chapter 2, once clients narrow their choices to their short list of top choices, they tend to choose providers who are client-centric instead of vendor-centric.

The Client-centric Assumption

Unlike the vendor and preferred provider, Third-Level providers work from the client-centric assumption that the more they know about their clients, the more likely they are to win the business.

Third-Level providers find out more (and care more) about their client's personal lives, their careers, and professional challenges above and beyond just the problems the service provider can solve. They know more about the unique characteristics of the property or project, the client's preferences, and decision process. They find and align to what is different about the client instead of forcing the client to find out what is different about them (see Figure 1.6).

Vendor-centric Vs. Client-centric

Vendor-centric Assumption: The more the client knows about me the more likely they are to choose me.
- Vendor does most of the talking
- Premature and non aligned solutions
- Looking to impress

Client-centric Assumption: The more I know about the client the more I can help them solve their problems and achieve their objectives.
- Partner listens more than talks
- Aligned with client
- Looking to help (Trust)

Figure 1.6 Enough About You.

Now think back to your last client meeting or presentation. Did the client do most of the talking? Was the content of your presentation or proposal mostly about the client's unique property, situation, concerns, and objectives? Were you a vendor, a preferred provider, or a strategic partner? If you acted as a strategic partner, you don't need to read this book, although you will certainly see yourself in it and may learn some ways to further enhance what you're already doing well. If, however, you're a vendor or a preferred provider, keep reading and you will learn to do the following:

- Identify and master the communication skills that elite providers employ to build strategic partnerships, win business, and retain committed clients

- Recognize why and how clients choose one real estate service provider over another
- Recognize that price decisions are frequently self-inflicted because price is the last of 10 choice factors
- Understand and align to predictable client decision patterns in order to reduce friction and enable faster choices
- Accelerate business relationships by learning how to engage clients in a strategic and client-centric level
- Accelerate client understanding, agreement, and commitment to your recommendations
- Position and present solutions that fit the client and beat the competition
- Build client preference for your solutions through a more differentiated rational and emotional value proposition
- Consistently get first and last look
- Get chosen away from price
- Win more and sell less

DELIBERATE PRACTICE: ARE GREAT SALES PEOPLE BORN OR MADE?

After I wrote my first book and began my consulting practice, I assumed that my best clients would be those who I could help the most. What surprised me was that the service providers who hired me tended to be those who needed me the least. They were already pretty darn good at acquiring and retaining clients. When I conduct training workshops, it is always the best performers coming in who get the most out of the class.

This taught me that the best professionals get that way because they have always been motivated to improve. Weaker providers don't improve because they are not aware that their poor skill performance is holding them back or because they lack motivation to go through the pain of improving. The best keep getting better. Tiger Woods is a good example.

A few years back he decided to change his grip, the way he holds his golf club. This is a radical move for a professional golfer. It can take months if not years to remaster your swing after this delicate but fundamental change. As a result, the next season was the worst of his career. Why did he do it? Simple, he thought he could be better. After recently winning six of seven tournaments he said, "One of the reasons I made the changes I made was to get to this point. And the great thing is we have a long way to go."

Over the years I have heard many potential client executives say that good salespeople are born, not made. The implication is that sales training may not be worth it. Either you were born to be an elite player or you weren't.

There is obviously some truth to this. But does that mean training is a waste of time?

According to an article in *Fortune* magazine, "What it takes to be great" (by Geoffrey Colvin, October 19, 2006), research conducted by Dr. Anders Ericsson now shows that the lack of natural talent is irrelevant to great success. Instead, painful and demanding practice and hard work separate the best from the rest. According to the article, people may use their innate characteristics to opt into or out of certain activities. For example, at 5' 8", I chose not to become an NBA star early on. However, once you have chosen a field or profession aligned with your gifts, effort is more important than innate talent.

Most accomplished people need around 10 years of hard work before becoming world class, a pattern so well established researchers call it the 10-year rule. Further, the best people in any field are those who devote the most hours to what the researchers call "deliberate practice": "activity that's explicitly intended to improve performance that reaches for objectives just beyond one's level of competence, provides feedback on results, and involves high levels of repetition," according to the article.

Of course understanding something and being able to do it are very different. You may agree with many of the principles of Third-Level Selling but find that you continue with your vendor-centric ways. That is because knowledge is much easier to change than behavior. For example, I read *Golf Digest*. I can describe the proper techniques for improving putting, but I am still a lousy putter. Why? I don't practice putting. I practice driving.

The bottom line is that you can dramatically improve your game, but you will need to practice each concept until you master it. Even if you believe that you are not a natural in sales, you can still lower your handicap. If you are a natural, deliberate practice could make you the best.

The objective of this book is not just to reveal what the elite providers do to build partnership. Instead I want to give you the tools and the practices that will take you from awareness to mastery. Therefore, each chapter concludes with ideas and tools you can use to develop a deliberate practice of the Third-Level Selling principles.

So I recommend that you do a quick read first. That will give the theory. But to build mastery you will need to treat this more like a workbook. Stop at the end of each chapter and diligently work through the suggested deliberate practice until you have mastered each step. The deliberate practice is the driving range. Keep working on each skill until you have grooved that portion of your game. Then move on to the next chapter and repeat.

If you put in the work, you can shorten your learning curve significantly. And the payoff is that you will win more and enjoy your career more. You will be chosen more often and work with friendlier and more committed clients who will end up selling for you. Good luck!

DELIBERATE PRACTICE FOR THIRD-LEVEL SELLING

Are You Selling Airbags? Read over your last proposal or listen to a colleague's presentation. Read or listen with client eyes and ears. Would this proposal or presentation convince you? Can or do your best competitors say about the same thing? If so, you are selling airbags: important but undifferentiated characteristics that don't really help clients choose you. What can you do to make your message more compelling?

Are You Vendor-centric or Client-centric? Do your proposals and presentations begin with information about your company, capabilities, experience, and so on (vendor-centric), or do they present unique information about this client's situation, problems, objectives, unique property characteristics, and client preferences (client-centric)? How could you make your message more client-centric?

Do You Have a Client-centric Attitude? Sometimes slight changes in attitude will naturally change behavior and yield better results. In your next client meeting, go in with the attitude that you want to find out everything you can about this person, threats to their company or their career, what is unique about the project, their preferences, and their decision process. Listen as much as possible. Talk as little as possible.

Chapter 2

How (and Why) Clients Choose You

Clients hire service providers to solve problems, and when they have choice, they choose providers who they feel can solve their problems better than the rest. In this chapter we explore decision patterns involved in the real estate service provider selection processes to prepare you to navigate and win in competition. The more you understand how and why clients are making these decisions the easier it will be to align and win.

Let's look at the service provider decision from the client's perspective. Let's say you were hired by one of your clients and assigned to a new city where you didn't know anyone. Your first assignment is to choose a service provider who does what you used to do. This is a very high-profile assignment. If you do it well, your hiring will be well justified. If it doesn't go well, you could be out on the street. How would you go about finding and then choosing a service provider? Remember, your job is on the line.

Just as your clients would, you will probably want to identify a number of alternatives and then have them compete for your business.

HOW CLIENTS CHOOSE YOU

Search: "Who Can Do It?"

The first thing you may do is try to identify who the service providers are in your new city who have the capabilities, approach, and experience that you are looking for. Let's say through research and references that you identified six potential providers. What now? Are you ready to make a decision? Who and how will you choose?

Screen: "Who Can Take Care of It Better?"

With so many choices you will probably want to get more information so you can determine who can take care of it better. So you ask those qualified providers to submit written information describing their capabilities, experience, approach, and fees. The more choice you have, the more selective you can be. Would you pick a winner from this group?

Perhaps if one provider was clearly superior to the rest, you could. For example, if one provider was the market leader and had done twice as much as his/her nearest competitor, you could go right to your final decision. But even with a clear capabilities leader, you will probably want to meet with the short list of the best two or three. After all, the vendor you choose can make or break your career, and you will be working closely with them for weeks or months.

Select: "Who Will Take Better Care of Me?"

Now that you have identified the most capable finalists, you can move to more subjective and emotional considerations: Who do you know, like, and trust the most? Which of the short listed providers knows you, your business, market, your situation, property, preferences, and decision process the best? Once you have narrowed the group to the few who can best take care of it, now you are looking for the one who will best take care of you.

The formal RFP (request for proposal) selection process can be pictured as a funnel with three phases, where criteria are used first to increase choice and then to eliminate alternatives until the final selection is made. The three phases of the service provider selection process are the search phase, the screening phase, and the selection phase.

Inclusion or exclusion in each phase is based on decision criteria that become increasingly selective and subjective. The number of provider candidates eventually narrows down to a single winner, as shown in Figure 2.1.

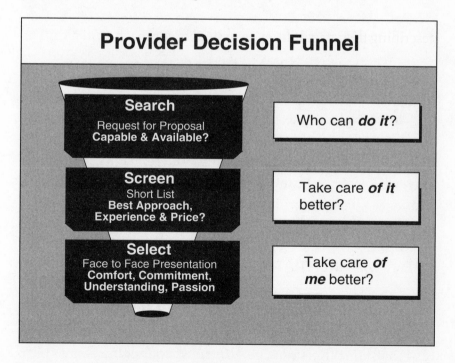

Figure 2.1 How Clients Choose You.

Decision Hierarchy

Client Differentiators
1. **Personal Relationship**
2. **Professional Relationship**
3. **Property/Project Difference**
4. **Preference Difference**
5. **Process Difference**

Vendor Differentiators
6. **Proof**
7. **Experience**
8. **Approach**
9. **Capabilities**
10. **Price**

Figure 2.2 Why Clients Choose You.

This complex process breaks down into client preferences driven by 10 differentiators that are listed in order of importance (see Figure 2.2). Although any one of these differentiators could determine who wins the business, relationship has the most influence, and, surprisingly, price has the least influence within a range.

CLIENT DIFFERENTIATORS

1. Personal Relationship: Who does the client know, like, and trust better?
2. Professional Relationship: Who understands the client's business, industry, market, company situation, and role better?

3. Project/Property: Who understands the client's project/property/market better?
4. Execution Preferences: Who understands the concerns, objectives, and visions of each client decision maker better?
5. Decision Process: Who better understands the client's decision process—who, when, and how the client will make the decision to choose a service provider?

VENDOR DIFFERENTIATORS

6. Proof (rank, stories, benchmarks, testimonials): Who does the client believe offers the best evidence?
7. Experience: Who does the client perceive presents the least risk?
8. Approach Difference: Who offers the best approach that others can't match?
9. Capabilities Difference: Who has a better capabilities fit for what the client is trying to do?
10. Price: Who offers the lowest price?

As you can see, the 10 differentiators are further broken down into client differentiators, what is different about the client, and vendor differentiators, what is different about you and your company when compared with your competitors. The vendor differentiators are important early on in the process when the client is assembling competitors, but become less significant as the client moves to a final decision.

Surprisingly, price is the least of 10 factors. I realize that this statement is highly controversial for those of you who have been beaten down by price lately, and I will discuss price in more detail in Chapter 10. However, within a range, price is only the deciding factor if the client perceives no difference up the hierarchy. The perception of price difference is in the eyes of the client. For some clients a penny is too much. Other clients may be willing to spend 10 percent to 15 percent more for their preferred provider.

When the client perceives a significant price difference, he or she may retrade the other factors to determine if the price difference is worth it to them. Once again, vendor differentiators like your capabilities or unique approach may be enough to win the business if the client doesn't have or want choice.

Occasionally one provider is able to offer capabilities or an approach that others can't match. But that advantage is unusual in the real estate services environment, and the advantage doesn't last long as competitors quickly copy each other's best practices.

Rank is the most powerful vendor differentiator. It is the metric that proves you have more experience than your competition. Again, if the client perceives that one provider dominates his or her competitors, that alone may be enough to carry the decision.

Service provider selections at this level expose decision makers to a great deal of career risk. If the chosen provider does not perform well, it could reflect negatively on the decision maker. In some cases it could torpedo a career. Decision makers are turning over the keys to their future to the service providers they choose; therefore, rank—who has done more than anyone else—plays a prominent role in the final choice. The market leader is the safest choice.

As Figure 2.3 shows, the client decision maker takes on more personal risk when choosing lower ranking providers. That is why market leaders tend to stay leaders. Companies frequently make the safe choice even when it is not the best choice.

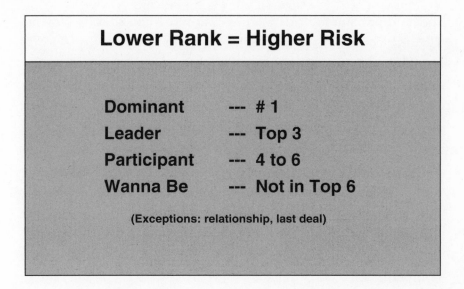

Figure 2.3 Why Winners Tend to Keep Winning.

This need to reduce risk gives market leaders a big advantage. If a company chooses the market leader and something goes wrong, it's the market leader's fault. But if a client executive takes the risk of not choosing the market leader and something goes wrong, it's perceived to be his or her fault for not making the safe choice. Dominant players get a hall pass to the short list every time. If you are not the market leader, the deck is always stacked against you.

The two exceptions to this rule are when one service provider did the last deal in this market, even if that provider is not the market leader, or one provider has a personal relationship with the client. The provider who did the last deal may know more about the current conditions in the market than even the dominant player. That gives them a temporary advantage. If you did the last deal, act on it quickly by contacting other potential clients in similar circumstances. Offer to share what you have learned as the quid pro quo for the meeting. If they are considering moving forward, you will have rank in their eyes.

The second exception to the higher rank rule is when a provider has a personal relationship with the client. As we will explore in later chapters, personal relationship is the biggest driver of choice among qualified alternatives. Clients prefer to work with someone they know even if that provider is not the best.

When you pitch or position your services, you are asking the client to learn what is different about your capabilities, approach, and experience (vendor differentiators). But once the client has narrowed his or her choice down to highly qualified alternatives, your capabilities look pretty much the same as your strongest competitors.

Differences among highly qualified providers can narrow to a thread, but there is plenty of room to differentiate on what is unique about the client (the client differentiators). If you know the client better, it's almost impossible for even the most capable competitors to unseat you.

STANDARD LIFE INVESTMENTS REAL ESTATE (SLIRE) EXAMPLE

After years of managing its own extensive and growing portfolio of 69 properties throughout Canada, Standard Life Investments (Real Estate) Inc. (SLIRE) signed an agreement with Colliers International to take on the management and leasing for their $350 million portfolio. The decision process that SLIRE used to find, screen, and select a service partner provides an excellent real world example of how clients choose among alternatives. And as we will see later, Colliers' approach to winning this project demonstrates how a Third-Level response will help you get chosen.

Let's take a closer look at how SLIRE worked through the decision funnel.

Search Phase: "Who can do it?"

Decision criteria during the search phase are inclusive and designed to gather as many alternatives as necessary to assure (and demonstrate) a good decision (see Figure 2.4). Inclusion is based on the client's awareness of providers with relevant capabilities and experience. Service providers will recognize the search phase as the RFP (request for proposal), RFI (request for information), or SOQ (statement of qualifications) stage of the process. The

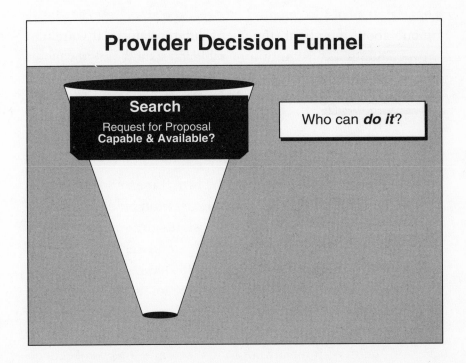

Figure 2.4 How Clients Create Their Invitation List.

client's objective is to maximize choice by including anyone who is potentially qualified to help.

SLIRE initially identified 10 companies who appeared to have the capabilities to handle the management and leasing of their investment portfolio. Peter Cuthbert, the SLIRE vice president who headed up the search, asked each of the 10 potential providers to respond to a request for information (RFI).

The stakes were high for Cuthbert and his team. If the third-party service providers did not perform well, it would have a serious impact on the careers of all concerned. Cuthbert said that SLIRE was "looking for a partner not just a vendor."

Screening Phase: "Who can take care of it better?"

The search phase frequently uncovers too many choices to be individually evaluated. The objective of the screening phase is to winnow the group down to a manageable "short list" for closer personal evaluation (see Figure 2.5). The screening phase is a rational comparison process where clients review written proposals. Standards for comparing similar characteristics are set, and these criteria are used to eliminate some potential vendors and establish preference among the remaining alternatives. Standards are tightened to eliminate all but the two, three, or four short list competitors who most closely align to decision criteria.

Criteria for new or infrequent decisions are constantly changing as clients learn more about their problems and potential solutions. For routine service provider selections, criteria tend to be more stable. Survivors of the screening phase often include the least risky (market leaders, incumbents, and other "safety buys") for reliability, the least expensive for price leverage, and the most innovative for idea leverage. Frequent service purchasers will often skip the first two phases and invite only the

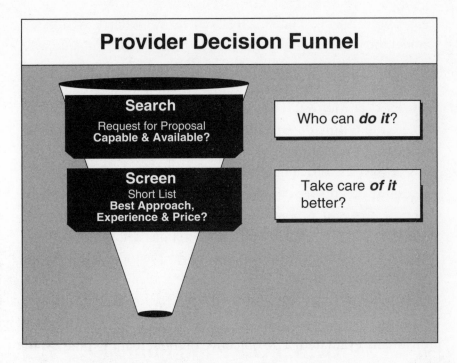

Figure 2.5 How Clients Choose Their Short List.

"short list" firms to speed the process, yet still negotiate the best terms.

According to Cuthbert at SLIRE, narrowing the list of alternatives from 10 down to six was easy. Four companies did not have the coverage to match up with a national portfolio. The SLIRE selection team kept narrowing vendor differentiation criteria to identify the best three to create a short list. The three short-listed companies were then asked to respond to a more detailed request for proposal (RFP) and invited to make presentations.

Selection Phase: "Who will take care of me better?"

The first two phases of the selection process are rational and, if done well, offer the prospect an opportunity to make a decision on a more subjective basis. The short list candidates are invited to meet the decision makers and present their cases. Anyone who has made it this far is well qualified, so decision criteria expand beyond capabilities to the unique rational and emotional fit of one provider over the rest. The criteria used to narrow the short list to the chosen provider are usually based on emotional reactions that include confidence, comfort, and trust (see Figure 2.6).

The service provider's demonstrated understanding of the unique aspects of the client and the project builds confidence. Comfort speaks to the personal compatibility of the provider and client. Do they like each other? Trust is elicited from the demonstrated commitment and experience to see the project through to a successful completion. These subjective attributes are impressions and are largely communicated non-verbally. If the purchaser

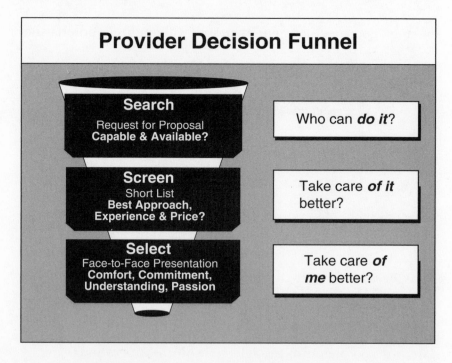

Figure 2.6 How Clients Pick the Winner.

perceives no differences between providers, low price will be used to determine the winner.

Standard Life screened the capable list down to a short list of preferred providers based upon the vendor differentiators. After the screening phase the list was shortened to three surviving companies that were invited to present their final proposals in the selection phase. As we will see later in the book, the winning bidder, Colliers, initially the dark horse in the competition, used a Third-Level approach to find and align to the client differentiators in order to win the selection phase.

Clients follow predictable patterns when choosing among alternatives. The more you understand why and how those decisions are made the more you can align your selling efforts and be chosen in competition. Clients will organize a competition to get information, leverage terms and price, and demonstrate that they are making a good decision. They will start with inclusive criteria and then narrow their choice to a short list to be evaluated in person.

Before we break down how competing providers advance from capable vendor to preferred provider in the next chapter, let's first discuss picking the right battles. One of the best ways to improve your win rate is to avoid battles where your chances are slim. Now that you have seen how and why clients choose one provider over another, it should be easier to pick battles where you have a shot. It's a bit like playing poker. If you know what cards your opponent is holding, you can make better decisions about when to hold 'em and when to fold 'em.

PICK YOUR BATTLES

To win in competitive situations you need to make more of an investment than updating a previous proposal with a new cover letter and different logos. Responding to an RFP typically drains a firm of 40 to 100 man-hours, but on larger projects it can balloon to hundreds of hours. Multiply those hours by salary and overhead and suddenly you have a very expensive investment. Instead of responding to every RFP that comes along, ask yourself whether you have the cards to go "all in."

The point is to look at the RFP response as an investment. What is the likelihood of winning? Would that time be better spent picking a better opportunity instead of taking a long shot on a beauty contest? To pick better battles, ask yourself the following questions (listed in Figure 2.7 on the following page).

If you answered "no" to two or more of these questions, particularly the first two, you may want to choose a better prospect, one who is better aligned with your value.

Pick Your Battles
(Do we have the cards to win?)

1. Do we have the *best relationship*?

2. Do we know the client's *project/property, preference, and process* better?

3. Are we *ranked* in the top 3?

4. Do we have and can we *prove* unique knowledge, approach, skills, capabilities, or resources that are critical to the project's success and difficult for competitors to copy?

5. Do we have *access* to the client before submission?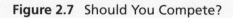

Figure 2.7 Should You Compete?

Use the time saved to differentiate on a new client or migrate an existing client to a new project. The investment is higher but so is the win rate. Now I will show you how to win the battles that you pick.

DELIBERATE PRACTICE: HOW (AND WHY) CLIENTS CHOOSE YOU

Diagnose Your Wins and Losses:

- Why did you win the last project you won?
- Why did you lose the last project you lost?
- Did those reasons fit the decision hierarchy presented in this chapter?
- How will your understanding of how and why clients choose service providers change the way you compete for their business?
- How will you move from capable to preferred provider to partner?

Pick Your Battles:

Think about a current competitive pursuit. Read your cards, and then read your competition's cards. Answer these questions to determine if you should compete:

- Do we have the best relationship?
- Do we know the client's project/property, preferences and process better?
- Are we ranked in the top three?
- Do we have and can we prove unique knowledge, skills, capabilities, approach, or resources that are critical

(Continued)

to the project's success and difficult for competitors to copy?

- Do we have access to the client before submission?

If you answered "no," particularly to the first two questions, you have probably already lost the business. Move on to a new opportunity. If you decide to compete, I will now show you how to improve your cards to give you the best chance of winning.

Chapter 3

Navigating From Vendor (Level 1) to Preferred Provider (Level 2)

Now that you know how client companies move through the real estate service provider selection process, I will now show you how to navigate the first two phases of the decision process and move from a qualified vendor to a preferred provider. The first step is to get invited.

SEARCH PHASE: LEVEL 1 - PITCH TO GET INVITED!

You did not choose your last car because it had wheels, an engine, brakes, radio, air conditioning, and so on. Of course the car had to have those things, but they are part of the basic package. When a client is looking for a service provider, they first need to establish that you have the basic package or capabilities before they start comparing you to others.

Your pitch is your offer to the entire market. It defines you at the broadest level. I am a broker, lender, contractor, designer, and so on. Your pitch is what gets you invited to compete in the first place. It answers the question, "Can you do it?" It establishes both your capability and credibility. It is your list of basic components (see Figure 3.1).

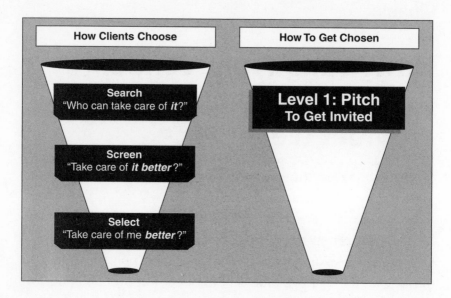

Figure 3.1 Pitch to Get Invited.

The Generalist Trap

You sell real estate services. And unlike products, a service does not exist when you sell it. The client can't drive it, taste it, or measure it. It is a promise to do something in the future, so it's hard for the client to make quality judgments with certainty in advance.

The good news is that you can change a service pitch on the fly to meet the unique needs of the client. Service providers can change their product to be "whatever the client wants." You need to lease an office building or sell your gas station? I can do that. You need to finance industrial space or a bowling alley? I can do that. You need landscaping for a mall or a warehouse? I can do that.

Unfortunately, that flexibility leads to what I call the "generalist trap." Real estate service providers too often define themselves as broadly as possible in order to get invited to more competitions. Although that strategy may work for your web site message and collateral material, it works against you in competition.

At a recent meeting I asked a broker where he specialized. He told me he specialized in office and industrial, multifamily, and retail sales and did both tenant and landlord leasing. Then I asked him what he did not specialize in. He had to think for a moment.

He explained that he had to define himself broadly because real estate asset classes went through cycles. When one asset class was down, he needed to be able to move quickly to another in order to survive. This generalist trap thinking is quite common in the real estate sector. You might get invited with a generalist message, but you won't win with it.

Think about it. When markets are down, do clients get more or less selective? Clearly the answer is that they get more selective because they have more choice. If I am a client in a tough market, and I have a choice between the generalist who has done a couple of these, a few of those, and some of the other, or the provider who has done 10 deals just like mine, who am I going to choose? Of course I will choose the specialist.

Based upon this broker's answer, it was clear why he was barely surviving. By trying to be everything to everybody, he ended up being nothing special to anyone. That is also why you see competitors using almost identical language in their proposals and presentations.

The majority of real estate providers never advance beyond Level 1 (the pitch). That is why most service providers are only surviving. That is also why the elite minority make the majority of the money.

SCREENING PHASE: LEVEL 2 - POSITION VERSUS COMPETITION

Perhaps 99 percent of what you do is the same as what your nearest competitor does. That means that the 1 percent difference drives

100 percent of choice. In competitive situations if a prospective client does not see or value even the smallest characteristics that make you better, it threatens your ability to win the business. That is why it is so important to identify and then position your differentiators (see Figure 3.2).

Yet even as clients move from the search to the screening phase of the selection process, most vendors are still pitching the same "airbags" that got them invited. Although still important, these characteristics are not perceived as different. They were the ante to play.

For example, one lender told the client they should choose him because his company had been in the business for 50 years. Why is that important to the client? If a competitive lender's company has been in the business for 10 years, what is the difference?

Jerry Anderson has held a number of executive positions for brokerage firms including president of Coldwell Banker Commercial and president of Sperry Van Ness' National Advisor

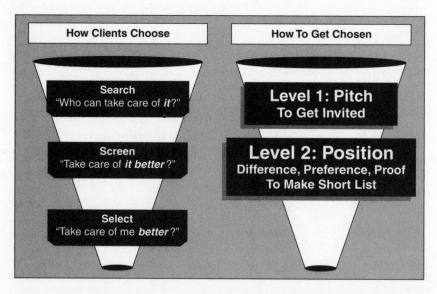

Figure 3.2 Position to Make the Short List.

Organization. As part of his screening process when hiring new brokers, he would ask them to pretend they were with a client and had to answer the following three questions: Why your company? Why you? Why now? According to Jerry, the majority of the answers were buzz phrases. Would you be able to answer those questions?

Most service providers can communicate why they should be chosen over the weakest competitors. But weaker players are weeded out early on during the screening phase. Now you are in the playoffs, and the competition is much tougher. Why should this client choose you over your best competitor?

How does a client determine who can get them the best outcome with the least risk, effort, and disruption when every service provider is saying the same thing? Is it any wonder vendors feel commoditized and are forced to compete on price?

To successfully position against competition you will want to determine your unique value zone, then craft a message that communicates what makes you different and better, and then prove it.

Specialize to Find Your Value Zone

Instead of trying to be all things to all clients, try to find and then communicate what you are best at. I call this your "value zone." You would be surprised how narrowly you can define your market and still make a great living.

We have all had the experiences, particularly early in our career, where we were talking to a potential client and thinking that we may be able to help them, but it's not really an area where we have had a lot of experience. At such times you know you are working outside of your value zone.

Every now and then, though, we find a client who has the problems that we solve and prefers the way that we solve them.

When that happens, it feels like you are running downhill. You know you are going to win this business because the client is clearly in your value zone. Why not find and then spend all of your business development efforts in your value zone?

The more you focus the more you can dominate your market. The more you dominate your market the easier it becomes for new clients to choose you (see Figure 3.3).

Where can you become dominant? Keep narrowing your market by asset type, size, geographic area, service, client situation, and so on, until you are at least in the top three. For example, one broker I worked with narrowed his target market to airport warehouses. Another specialized in "green" buildings. Once you have specialized, then you can work on differentiating your message.

During the screening phase, your value narrows to differentiators—what the client perceives you do better than your best competitor. Further, it is not enough just to be better, it must also be important to the client. For example, your company may have a global platform that others don't have, but frankly most local

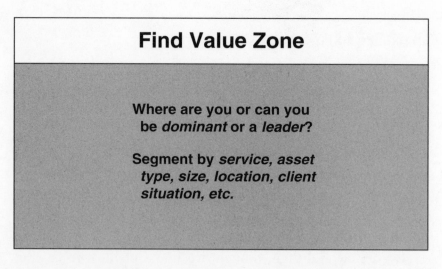

Figure 3.3 Clients Prefer to Work with #1.

Airbag or Differentiator?

Airbag?

- **Others can and do say it**
- **Does not help the client choose**

Differentiator?

- **Provable Difference**
- **Important to client**
(Solves a stated problem)

Figure 3.4 What Are Your Differentiators?

clients don't care about that. It may be a difference, but because it is not important to the client, it doesn't create preference so it is not a differentiator (see Figure 3.4).

To summarize, a differentiator must have two characteristics:

1. It must be perceived as different and better.
2. It must be important to the client. That is it must address this client's stated concern or objective.

POSITION DIFFERENCE, PREFERENCE, AND PROOF

To define your differentiators within your value zone, first identify what could go wrong because that sets the selection criteria a client will use to compare you to alternatives. Selection criteria will usually focus on the reliability of execution because at this level the client is effectively asking, "Who can most reliably deliver us from where we are now to where we want to be?"

Map out the execution process. Where are the usual points of friction? What are the mistakes that inexperienced providers are likely to make that more experienced providers wouldn't? How would those mistakes impact the client? What is most likely to increase client risk? What adds to the client's workload? What causes delays, disruption, and cost overruns?

To "de-airbag" and separate your offer from your best competitor clearly articulate your difference, preference, and proof for each client execution objective. What is different about your capabilities, experience, or approach? Why should that difference create preference? What is your proof that you can do it better? Start with the objective and then outline your differentiators. It should flow like this:

- Objective: What is the client's primary stated execution concern or objective?
- Description: What do you do better to reduce that risk or achieve that objective?
- Difference: What is different about your idea, service, approach, process, or system?
- Preference: Why should that difference create preference? Why is it important to the client?
- Proof: Why should a client believe you? What is your proof? Even if two vendors say the same thing, the one who can prove it will win.

Prove It to Make the Short List

Proof is the most important part of your message. Remember a service does not exist when it is sold. It is a promise to do something

Positioning Proof

1. **Story:** *Previous client in similar situation*

2. **Benchmark:** *Metric that shows better outcome*

3. **Testimonial:** *Specific client comment that speaks to how your difference achieved benchmark*

Figure 3.5 Why Should the Client Believe You?

in the future. That uncertainty reduces your value in the mind of a client who has not worked with you before. Do you have any evidence or proof that this client will get the results that your difference offers? If you are better, there is always proof: a story, a metric, and/or a testimonial. The more evidence that you have that you can achieve the outcome or reduce the risk, the more likely you will be chosen (see Figure 3.5).

A good proof statement will carry the majority of the argument and accelerate your positioning message. The best proof statements have three components:

1. A **relevant story** or anecdote about another client in a similar position
2. A **benchmark** or metric that demonstrates a better outcome
3. A **specific client testimonial** that speaks to how your differentiator uniquely contributed to the better outcome.

Look at these two responses given to a client looking for a broker to sell a property. The client's objective was to sell the property quickly because they wanted the cash to purchase another property in a different market. Who would you choose?

Broker 1: "We can do it faster because we know who is in the market and we have a lot of experience with this type of asset. We can get you testimonials from other clients."

Broker 2: "We can get you the fastest execution because we will use our private investor execution. *It's different because* where most brokers slowly roll out the property to a narrow market in order to protect their commission, we will immediately show this property not only to our database of buyers, but also to all internal and external brokers and share commissions. *That is important to you because* it attracts the most buyers quickly. It puts pressure on the buyers to move faster because they know another buyer is standing in the wings. *For example,* we recently inherited a property form another brokerage firm that had been on the market for six months. Using our private investor execution, we found a buyer in three weeks. That buyer was from another city and was brought in by another firm. The seller told us that our fast and open execution "saved my job. My only regret is that we did not know about you six months ago."

Where the first broker offered vague airbags, the second broker offered specific and relevant vendor differentiators—difference, preference, and proof.

- Client's execution objective: Fast execution for liquidity
- Broker's unique offer: Private investor execution

- Difference: Full market exposure, shared commission versus sequential pocket listing
- Preference: Early full exposure brings the market sooner and creates competition and seller leverage
- Proof:
  1. Story: Similar property on the market for six months
  2. Benchmark: Three weeks versus six months or more
  3. Testimonial: "Saved my job."

HARVESTING SPECIFIC TESTIMONIALS

When I ask participants in my workshops to bring a proof statement to the class, they will usually offer their pitch and then say, "We can get you testimonials from other clients." That's not proof. It is a vague offer to get something later. The client is trying to make a decision now. They either have to wait to make a decision until after they get your proof or, more likely, make a decision based upon the airbag message that you have already offered. Do you really want to risk this client decision on such flimsy evidence?

The offer to get something to the client later leaves the most important part of your positioning statement devoid of a punch line. How much easier would it be for this client to choose you now if you had compelling proof ready to present? Help your clients choose you by offering your best proof now.

Generally clients don't offer testimonials. You need to ask for them. Most testimonials are in the form of letters. They are almost always vague and general: "Jennifer is great. We really enjoyed working with her." That's not proof. Everyone can offer the pro forma testimonial letter. Your proof statement should speak directly to this client's objective and show that your difference helped another client in similar circumstances achieve their objective better.

The best way to harvest a specific testimonial is to offer to write it yourself. First, ask a recent client how your participation in the transaction helped them achieve their objectives. Assuming they give you a positive answer, ask if you can use their statement as a testimonial for new clients. Then offer to write up what you heard them say and show it to them for review.

Your offer to craft the testimonial does two things: It reduces your client's workload, which means it will get done faster, and second, it gives you editorial control of the comment. You can write it so that it makes a good specific testimonial. Clients will usually accept your suggested script as you wrote it. Then you can offer new clients real proof. That will make it far easier for them to choose you.

RANK AS PROOF

In my experience clients are much more interested in not making a mistake and looking foolish than they are in optimizing results. At the intersection of greed and fear, fear almost always has the right of way. As we presented earlier, the safest choice in any service provider decision is to go with the market leader. Therefore your rank is one of the most powerful proofs you can offer to a client, and the higher the rank the safer the choice. The lower the rank of the service provider the more risk the decision maker takes on.

One broker I worked with told me she was one of the top players in the downtown retail market. When I asked her if she had proof, she said that she did not but that she could probably get it. The next week she produced a bar graph that showed her market share was three times higher than her nearest competitor. Imagine how much easier it is for a client to choose her after looking at that chart than when she simply said she was the market leader.

Proof is the key to differentiation. If two providers say the same thing but one can prove it, the provider who can prove it will win every time.

EXPERIENCE IS SIMPLY THE NAME WE GIVE OUR MISTAKES. (OSCAR WILDE)

By far the most common answer given by service providers as to why a client should choose them is because of their track record: "You should choose me because of my experience." Because clients hear that so often the words lose traction and fail to create preference. What does experience mean? Why is it important to this client? How is your experience different?

Experience is what you have learned usually from the accumulation of mistakes made at the expense of previous clients. In effect clients pay for the education of inexperienced providers because they are victims of the mistakes that more experienced providers can inoculate against.

Certain common mistakes are predictable to the experienced provider. Experienced providers can see them coming and know how to avoid them. However, unforeseeable problems inevitably arise in any project. There again, experienced professionals seem to know how to work their way through even unforeseen problems better.

BCCI is a very successful San Francisco-based commercial contractor. Here is how BCCI describes their experience in the context of a client execution concerns:

BCCI delivers superior results because controllable delays and disruptions that blow up budgets and schedules don't happen on our projects, so the client doesn't hear about material delays, permit

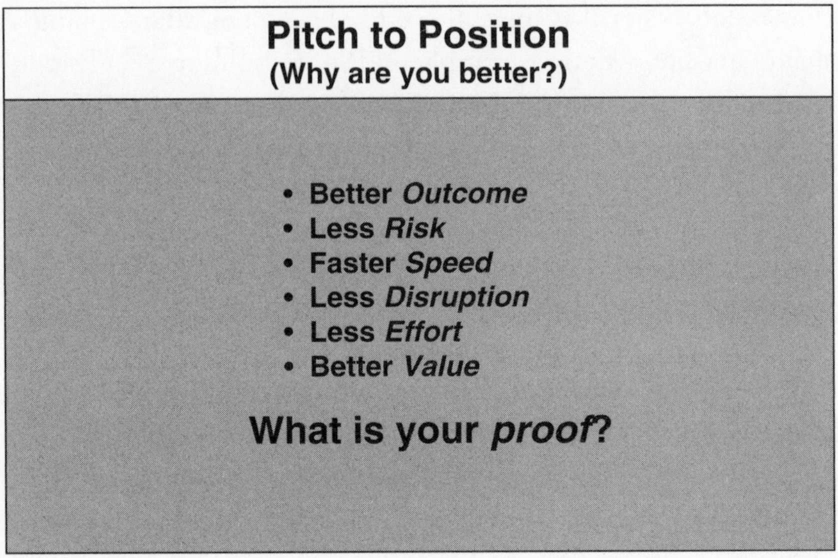

Pitch to Position
(Why are you better?)

- Better *Outcome*
- Less *Risk*
- Faster *Speed*
- Less *Disruption*
- Less *Effort*
- Better *Value*

What is your *proof*?

Figure 3.6 What Do You Do Differently and Better?

hang-ups, labor mismanagement, or uncoordinated workflow. Uncontrollable surprises are contained, that means the client is informed in a professional and collaborative manner.

(Several years ago I worked with BCCI to reengineer their market value proposition. If you would like to see a strong market offer from a commercial contractor, see Appendix 1 at the back of the book.)

Let's take a closer look at the other typical client execution objectives and concerns so that you can craft and prove your vendor differentiators (see Figure 3.6).

BEST OUTCOME

All clients want to get the best possible outcome. That usually means the best price and terms. What is the best possible outcome for your client?

For an investor selling an asset, the best outcome is almost always to get the best price. For the client of design services, the best outcome may be related to image and function. For the retail client looking to lease new space, the best outcome may be location and income producing potential. For the building owner it is higher rents and tenant retention. For the borrower, it is terms and conditions. How do you communicate to clients that you can uniquely help them achieve the best outcome?

However, most clients are more interested in reducing risk than getting the last possible penny out of the deal. At this point the problems that concern clients most are usually execution concerns and objectives. Who can help me get the best outcome the fastest with the least risk, effort, disruption, and cost? Who will make them look good to the market, their colleagues, and constituents?

Least Risk

If the outcome is in any way threatened, it won't matter who is offering the lowest price. Saving a few basis points means little if the deal craters. What is the biggest threat to the outcome of this transaction? What do you do to reduce that risk? How is that different and better than what you best competitor does? Can you prove it?

Least Work

Workload is frequently a hidden but very important execution concern. Your client has a day job. Ideally they want to hire someone in whom they have the confidence to let handle all of the extra work caused by going through with this project. The more the client feels they can trust you to handle everything the more likely you are to win.

For example, clients hire a third-party property manager because the client does not have the time or the expertise to manage the property themselves. Financing clients hate all of the seemingly unnecessary paperwork caused by documents prepared by the underwriting and legal departments, who are out to protect the company's balance sheet not make the client's application process easier.

Map the client's potential workload in your process. What can you or do you do to reduce that workload? How is that different from the way your best competitors handle it? Do you have any stories, benchmarks, and specific testimonials that prove that you're better at reducing your client's burden?

Faster

By the time the client makes a decision to go ahead with the project, time is almost always a key driver. Once they decide to sell a property, they want the transaction to occur as fast as possible so that they are not exposed to market risk and so they can have their money to make other investments that they deem better at this time.

What can you or do you do better to accelerate the process? Once again, how is that different than your best competitors? Why is that difference important to the client? What evidence do you have to prove it?

Disruption and Surprises

Most clients are more interested in predictability than they are optimal outcome. For example, the office manager at a law firm is more interested in minimizing disruptions to the partners than saving a few dollars on tenant improvements. When things don't go as planned, your client looks bad to his or her constituents. The more you can offer certainty and predictability of outcome, the more likely the client is to choose you because you can protect them from looking bad. One of my commercial contractor clients won a very large hospital seismic retrofit project because of their detailed plan to avoid disruption to the ongoing operations of the hospital during construction.

What is your difference, preference, and proof that your approach reduces disruption and surprises for your client? Consider these questions both from your company's perspective and from your perspective as the service provider. What is unique about your company? What is unique about you? Isolate and, whenever possible, name (brand) that unique capability. Naming it or giving it a brand further distinguishes this characteristic from competitive alternatives and makes it easier for potential clients to remember you.

CONGRATULATIONS! YOU MADE THE SHORT LIST OF PREFERRED PROVIDERS

So far the competition has been about you and your competitors. If you look again at the ten differentiators, you will notice that all of our work so far has been to improve your vendor differentiators (see Figure 3.7).

Price is the differentiator we would like to avoid. Capabilities and credibility are the antes to play. Your approach and experience could be key factors in the client's choice but only if they can't be matched. Your difference, preference, and proof accelerate and position your message and make it easier for the clients to choose you. And if the client does not already have a relationship with a provider who knows their property, preferences, and

Decision Hierarchy

Client Differentiators: 3rd Level

1. **Personal Relationship**
2. **Professional Relationship**
3. **Property/Project Difference**
4. **Preference Difference**
5. **Process Difference**

Vendor Differentiators: 2nd Level

6. **Proof**
7. **Experience**
8. **Approach**
9. **Capabilities**
10. **Price**

Figure 3.7 Vendor Differentiators Get You to the Short List.

processes better, then the provider with the most proof (usually rank) wins.

If you reach the selection phase as a preferred provider, it is because you have successfully differentiated your capabilities, approach, and experience from those service providers who were screened out. One or all of the following vendor differentiators got you here:

- Proof: You offered more proof in the form of rank, stories, benchmarks, or client testimonials.
- Experience: The client perceived that you were more reliable because you had the most experience.
- Approach: You offered a better approach that others couldn't match.

- Capabilities Difference: Your capabilities were perceived to be a better fit.
- Price: You offered the lowest price.

Starting with the next section, we will focus on the biggest drivers of choice: the client differentiators. Once we have uncovered what is unique about the client, you will see the power of aligning your vendor differentiators to fit that client.

To summarize, increased competition has probably obscured your value in the marketplace. Your inability to clearly see, communicate, and prove that you are different and better than competitors makes winning critical pursuits that much harder. If you can't see it and say it, how does your client see it and value it? How do they choose you?

On the other hand an accelerated positioning message not only makes it easier for clients to choose you, it also becomes a self-fulfilling prophesy as you dedicate resources to reinforce the characteristics that make you different and better. That builds your business, and it builds the morale of your staff as they increasingly feel part of a unique and winning team.

(If you would like to see an example where I helped a real estate company accelerate its value proposition, see Appendix 2.)

DELIBERATE PRACTICE: FROM VENDOR TO PREFERRED PROVIDER

Specialize to Dominate Your Value Zone:

Remember it is better to hold 50 percent of one market than 10 percent of five markets. Where can you be a dominant or leading player? Segment your market by:

- Service/product
- Asset type
- Size
- Location
- Client situation, and so on.

Keep narrowing until you can say you do more of this than anyone else. What is your market share? Can you create a bar chart to compare yourself with your competitors? If so, it will make it easier to choose you. Is that market big enough to make a living if you dominate it?

Position Difference, Preference, and Proof

- Map out the execution process from the client's perspective. Identify the major execution concerns and objectives that your clients are likely to have when choosing among capable service providers.
- Most clients are looking to get the best outcome with the least effort, disruption, and time commitment. For each of these concerns and objectives identify what you do or could do to address them better than your best competitors.

- Find proof. This is often the hardest part of accelerating your message, but it is by far the most important. If you do it better, there is proof. What stories do you have? What measurable results did you achieve? What did those clients say? (If you don't have a testimonial, go back to those clients and ask them and then ask if you could use their response in a testimonial. Even if they won't let you use their names, you can still say, "One of my clients said this.")

- Use the following template to script your statement. This may seem remedial until you try it. It forces you to clearly craft the key points of your message.

  You said your objective was to . . .
  We can help you do that better because . . .
  It is different because . . .
  That is important because . . .
  For example . . .

- Now practice your message until it sounds natural in conversation.

PART II

Third Level: From Preferred Provider to Chosen Partner

Now you are a finalist in the competition. You have made it to the red zone where the competition gets intense. All of the service providers on the short list are well qualified, so your professional qualifications probably won't differentiate you as much during this final stage.

The winner of the selection phase will be the provider that best establishes a partnership (Partner: Level 3) by differentiating on the client.

CLIENT EYES

Let's look again at the service provider choice from the client's eyes to understand why Third-Level Selling is critical to winning in competition. Let's say you need to hire someone to help you perform a critical task. We're not talking about fixing your sink or cutting your lawn here. If the service provider you hire doesn't perform, it could have dire consequences on your career. You've narrowed the list down to what you consider the best three. Now how do you choose among three?

You're going to be working closely with your service provider so you probably want to work with someone that you already know. You'll want to hire someone who can do this job at least as

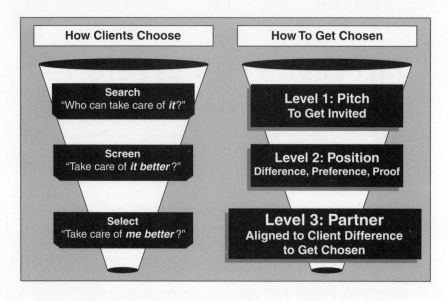

Figure PII.1 Differentiate on the Client to Build Partnership.

well if not better than you can. That means you want someone who already understands your industry, market, company, role, situation, and objectives. You don't want to have to spend a lot of time bringing them up to speed (see Figure PII.1).

Next it would be very helpful if your service partner had a deep understanding of your market, your project, or your property. If they understand the property better than anyone else, they will be able to use that information to your advantage. After all anyone can access research to determine comparable values. You want someone who can find out what is unique and leverage that to your advantage.

Next you would want someone who understands your preferences: how you like to work, what concerns you have that could threaten this project, and your vision of the best approach and likely outcome. You also want your service provider to be able to at least match the capabilities of competitive alternatives. Finally you want your service provider partner to understand and align to other decision makers and your decision process.

To summarize, here are the five client differentiators that clients use to choose among highly qualified service providers:

1. Personal Relationship: Who do I know, like, and trust the most?

2. Professional Relationship: Who understands me, my business, market, competition, threats, and opportunities the best?

3. Project/property/market difference: Which provider best understands what is unique about my project or property and market and can leverage that information to achieve the best outcome for me?

4. Preferences: Who best understands my concerns and unique execution preferences for achieving the best price with the lowest risk, effort, and disruption?

5. Decision process: Who understands our decision process—who, why, and how we make our decisions?

Third Level

Client Differentiators

1. Personal Relationship
2. Professional Relationship
3. Property/Project Difference
4. Preference Difference
5. Process Difference

Figure PII.2 What Makes This Client Different?

As you can see, when choosing a service provider, considerations go well beyond capabilities (see Figure PII.2). Clients are looking for someone who will not only take care of *it*, but someone who will take care of *them*—someone who will take this burden from their shoulders.

You don't sell a standardized product, and you don't sell to a mass market. Each prospect has different objectives, obstacles, personality, decision processes, resources, experiences, and deadlines. If you are going to be their partner, prospects want you to understand their unique circumstances; they want you to be personally invested in their objectives. Your knowledge of the client and his or her particular situation demonstrates commitment and builds comfort and trust.

Unfortunately, many service providers still treat their service and their potential clients alike. They customize their PowerPoint slides by adding prospect logos to their boilerplate vendor-centric presentations and then wonder why they lose or compete on price. They try to fit the client to the message.

Now think about how you sell your services. Are you simply presenting your capabilities and leaving it to the client to determine if those are valuable? (Level 1) Are you helping the client see what is different and better about your capabilities as compared with your best competitors? (Level 2) Are you doing what elite providers do, which is to develop a deep understanding of the client and then align your services and capabilities to assume your client's burden?

In the chapters that follow, I will break down each of these five client differentiators and show you why each is important and how elite service providers find and align to them (see Figure PII.3). Here is a summary of what we will cover:

1. Personal Relationship Acceleration: Finding personal common ground.

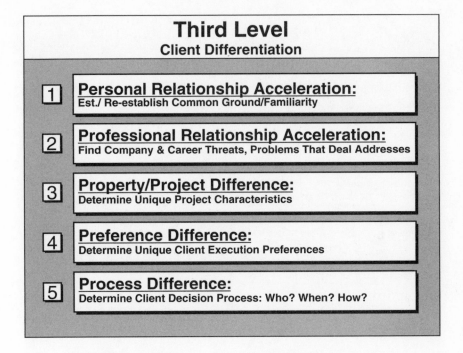

Figure PII.3 Third-Level Client Differentiation.

2. Professional Relationship Acceleration: Find threats to the client's career or company.

3. Project/Property/Market Difference: Find and align to what is unique about the project/property or market.

4. Preference Difference: Find and align to what is unique about this client's execution preferences related to outcome, risk, effort, timing, and disruption.

5. Process Difference: Find and align to what is unique about this client's decision process.

The objective is to migrate from a preferred provider into a full partnership with your clients. The first and most important step is to accelerate your personal relationships with clients. As we will explore in the next chapter, personal relationship is the single biggest driver of choice among capable alternatives.

DELIBERATE PRACTICE: THIRD-LEVEL CLIENT PROFILE

Take a current competitive pursuit for a new client to fill out the following Third-Level Client Profile to see how well you are uncovering client differentiators now.

Third Level™ Client Profile

1. **Personal: Common Ground?**
   Personal Client Info: (Time in position, previous, family, schooling, interests, common ground, etc.)

2. **Professional: Strategic and Deal-Related Problems?**
   Client Perception of Key Changes:

   Client Strategic Problems that could threaten career or company:

   Key real estate problem or objective you could support: How:

3. **Project/Property Difference?**
   Unique Project/Property Characteristics that impact risk, price, timing, execution:

4. **Preferences Difference?**
   Previous Experience, Concerns, Client's Visions, Competition:

5. **Client Decision Process?** (Timing, People, Decision Process?)

   Your Proof Statements For This Client?: Difference, Preference, Proof?

   Decision Stage and Momentum Recommendation:

Don't worry if you don't have a clear understanding of what I am asking for on the profile. In later chapters, I will go into detail in each of these areas.

Third-Level Diagnostic

Where are the gaps in your information in this client profile? Do you actually have common ground with the decision-maker or do you just know certain things about their personal background? Do you know what your client's perceptions are of the changes in their industry and market and threats to their career and company, or do you just have a general understanding of the industry? Do you know what separates this project or property and makes it different from similar properties, or do you just know the asset class and comparable values? Do you know specifically what this client's execution concerns are, or are you assuming they have the same concerns as all of your clients? What was their previous positive or negative experience? Did you capture their vision and expectations for outcome and approach? Do you know who you're competing with and what your client's perceptions of your relative strengths and weaknesses are? Do you know who else will be involved in this decision, what their roles will be, what their timing is, and what the decision process is?

If you were able to capture rich and unique information on your client in each of these five categories, you are already working at the Third Level. Congratulations! You have greatly enhanced your chances of winning. If there are gaps in your understanding of this client, keep reading and learn how elite providers differentiate on the client.

Chapter 4

Accelerating Personal Relationships

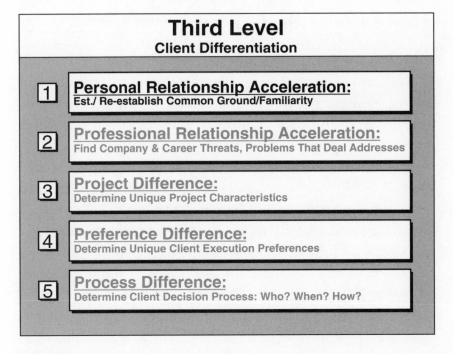

Third Level
Client Differentiation

1. **Personal Relationship Acceleration:**
Est./ Re-establish Common Ground/Familiarity

2. **Professional Relationship Acceleration:**
Find Company & Career Threats, Problems That Deal Addresses

3. **Project Difference:**
Determine Unique Project Characteristics

4. **Preference Difference:**
Determine Unique Client Execution Preferences

5. **Process Difference:**
Determine Client Decision Process: Who? When? How?

Figure 4.1 Find Common Ground to Accelerate Personal Relationships.

When clients need a service provider, they typically start with the familiar and then work their way out. They ask:

- *Can we do it?* This is the make or buy decision.
- *Can someone we know do it?* I call this the incumbent decision. Generally clients prefer to work with someone they have

67

worked with before. The demon they know is better than the demon they don't know. The more often the client is in the market, the more likely it is that they already have a preferred provider who will win the business unless they really screw up.

- *Do we know someone who knows someone who can do it?* This is the referral decision. The client would prefer to use the research and judgment of a trusted adviser to shorten the search and choice process. That is why it is critical to delight your existing clients. They become part of your personal sales force going forward.

Familiarity is, in fact, the single most important consideration when choosing a service provider among the short list of highly capable alternatives. Think about the last time you retained a service provider, perhaps your lawyer, tax or estate planner, or investment advisor. Did you conduct a request for proposal (RFP) process? Not likely. You probably picked someone you already knew. Both my attorney and tax accountant were college classmates. I played baseball with my investment manager. Are there providers who have better credentials? Sure. Could I get these services performed at lower fees? Probably. Would I change providers? Nope.

The reason we choose people close to us to provide key services is that we trust them more. We want to choose providers who are emotionally aligned with us because they understand our motivation, share our vision, and are often personally committed to helping us reach that vision. Although you would not retain a good friend if that person were not qualified, the people you know and trust have a distinct advantage over even those with potentially stronger capabilities.

How important is relationship in choosing a service provider? To find out, I surveyed more than 600 professionals about the

| **Relationship Effect** |
| "It's Personal" |
| **Relationship increases** |
| **"win rate"** |
| **200% to 300%** |

Figure 4.2 Personal Relationship Is the Most Powerful Driver of Choice.

influence of relationship in winning new business in competition and found that existing relationships increased win rates in competition by 200 percent to 300 percent.

No other factor (capabilities, experience, price, industry knowledge, etc.) came close as a choice influencer. As I will explore in Chapter 11, personal relationships separate satisfied clients from highly satisfied clients. Highly satisfied clients are twice as likely to repeat as clients who rate themselves as simply satisfied. Finally, personal relationships offer a distinct advantage when negotiating, as I will show you in Chapter 10.

Yet most providers either make no effort to improve their personal relationship with clients or leave it to chance. They assume that if they do a good job, the relationship will take care of itself.

The fact that relationship influences choice is no surprise. Assuming similar capabilities, don't you want to work with someone you already know? In my Third-Level seminars when I ask how many in the group believe that relationship is an important factor when a client chooses among competitive alternatives, all hands go up.

Interestingly though when I ask how many in the group have a proactive strategy for accelerating client relationships, almost no hands go up. When I further question those few who raise their hands as to how they accelerate their personal relationships with clients, they generally describe an ad hoc approach of looking for pictures on the desk or talking about the weather to prompt a discussion.

Providers frequently avoid personal conversation particularly early on because they feel clients are too busy for small talk or that it is inappropriate to get personal until later. But when you consider that it is the biggest driver of choice, you will want to make it a more systematic and proactive part of your client acquisition strategy.

You probably have a few clients that you would at least consider acquaintances, if not friends. These are people who you know and like, and they are people who know and like you and appreciate the value you bring to the table.

How much different is that from the cold call contact? For most service providers cold calling is the least attractive part of the job. That's because these new potential clients don't know you, don't know how you're different, and don't appreciate your unique capabilities. Whenever you meet a new client, there seems to be adversarial tension. You are the vendor, and they are the client. You can sense their resistance and even distrust.

I've met many a young broker who will proudly tell me that they make 100 cold calls every single day. Although I respect their work ethic, I personally would prefer to work for friends and acquaintances. That's why elite service providers work so hard to accelerate and maintain the relationships they have and then leverage those relationships to access new clients whenever possible.

FIND COMMON GROUND TO ACCELERATE RELATIONSHIPS

Relationships are based on common ground. Accelerating a personal relationship is a matter of finding that common ground between the client and you. And here's the secret: Finding common ground, even with a prospect you're meeting for the first time, is easy because the two of you inhabit a small world.

No doubt you're familiar with the idea of "six degrees of separation": that any two individuals in the world are connected by, at most, six others. A gondolier in Venice and an ivory carver in British Columbia. The barista at your local Starbucks and the Queen of England. You and Angelina Jolie. You know someone who knows someone who knows someone and so forth, and at most, there are only six someones between you and her.

When it comes to finding common ground with your clients, the world is much smaller. Chances are you and every one of your clients have a similar demographic profile: a specific geographic area, experience in real estate industry, a general level of education and income. Given all that, it's highly probable—in my experience it's virtually certain—that you have something in common the moment you meet. You're probably joined not by six degrees of separation, but by one.

THE RELATIONSHIP GAME: THREE TO FIVE QUESTIONS TO UNCOVER "AMAZING STORIES"

What question would you ask to find common ground? In my seminars I tell participants that they can usually find common ground by asking three to five questions that take a total or

30 seconds to ask. With any new or existing client try to ask the following questions:

1. How long have you been in this position?
2. What did you do before?
3. Did you grow up and do your schooling here?
4. Do you live in the area?

These work well for me, but you may develop better ones. Any one of these questions could lead to a longer discussion. It's a bit like playing the game Battleship where opponents can't see the location of the other's ship, but when one pegs a hit on the other's ship, they keep locating pegs around that spot until the opponent's ship is sunk. When one of these questions yields potential common ground, ask follow-up questions until you can feedback something that you have in common.

I recently had a telephone conversation with a potential new client. Although I had worked with his organization previously, this person was the new head of sales and had his own preferred vendors and so was a bit skeptical when we first started talking. Although he was about 10 years younger than I, and we live 2,000 miles apart, we were able to quickly find common ground using my four relationship acceleration questions above.

I found out that we both went to New Trier East High School near Chicago. He lives in Glencoe, which is the town where I grew up and where my parents still live only a few blocks away from him. Both his father and brother were graduates of Notre Dame as are my father and brother. In a matter of just a few minutes a potentially adversarial and awkward discussion became comfortable and friendly. As a result, I was able to retain this client.

Sometimes it helps if you share some of your personal information first and then ask your common ground questions. I ask training participants to try their three to five questions on prospects and clients, and report back at the next session. In most cases participants will comes back with an "amazing story":

"We grew up on opposite coasts, but it turns out he went to college with one of my oldest friends in the industry."

"We play in the same charity golf tournament every year."

"I couldn't believe it: my brother-in-law is best friends with this client's regular tennis partner. They all play doubles together a few times a year. He's even been to a cookout at my sister's house."

"We found out we grew up in the same town. It was half an hour before we finally got around to talking business!"

"Our kids went through preschool together."

Just below the service of every business relationship there is personal relationship based upon common ground. That common ground creates a deeper relationship, which in turn creates a powerful driver or preference for you over other service providers where there is only a vendor relationship.

Even when the client has an existing relationship with another provider, it can only help to accelerate your own relationship through common ground.

Find Common Ground Before You Meet

Frequently you can find quite a bit of personal and professional information by doing a search on your prospective client or by going to the company web site before the meeting or call. You can typically find professional profiles and biographies. You can determine where they're from and where they went to school. Use that information as a starting point and accelerate your relationship from there.

Soon your amazing stories become routine as you find you have something in common with most business contacts. And every one can serve as the foundation for accelerating your personal relationship with the client. Once you and a client discover that you have a mutual friend, went to the same school, live in the same town, share a certain experience or interest, it changes the nature of every interaction you have from then on. The adversarial nature of the vendor/client relationship recedes. Your meetings become friendly conversations between acquaintances, or even friends.

That makes it easier to find and align to the other client differentiators. Clients will be more willing to share their problems, objectives, and preferences and explore your solutions. Building your personal relationships in the professional world helps you win more, it helps you retain your clients better, and perhaps most importantly, it makes your job more fun.

Dangerous Questions

As we said in a previous chapter, experience is the accumulation of previous mistakes. With that in mind there are certain questions that may blow up in your face:

- *Where did you go to college?* "I didn't." You will notice that I modified this one to ask, "Where did you do your schooling?" I will leave it to the client to focus on high school, college, or post-graduate work.
- *Do you have kids? Are you married?* It turns out that these can be sensitive questions for couples who have tried unsuccessfully to have children or, God forbid, lost one. Someone who has recently gone through a bitter divorce or has never married will view these questions as intrusive.
- Questions about religion and politics are usually out of bounds, although one of my clients had good success accelerating a relationship when he found out that the client and he went to the same church.

Maintaining and Deepening Relationships

Real estate is a particularly collegial industry because it has to be. Every deal involves many players from different firms and professions. Owners, users, brokers, designers, engineers, builders, lenders, furnishers all have to work together to make the deal work. The elite players seem to know everybody in their area of specialization. They not only work together, they frequently hang together as well.

I discovered that this is a common trait for the high-level performers. I am not sure how you teach likability, but I am sure it starts with your liking other people. These elite players don't just participate in a network, they help create and maintain it. They tend to be the ones who organize events and start and are active participants in associations. They love to teach, mentor, and share best practices. It seems the business is an avocation to them.

Dan Winey, a managing principal at Gensler, one of the premier architectural firms, is a master networker, not because he has to be, but because he wants to be. He not only loves the business, he loves the participants. Dan seems to know and socialize with everyone associated with the San Francisco real estate community. I first met Dan at a Scotland golf outing that he had organized for a number of friends from the industry.

When I interviewed Dan for the book, every question led to a list of market-leading names for me to talk to. Every time I brought up a subject, Dan brought out his Blackberry, looked up a name, and directed me to talk to his good friend so and so. He even gave me the names of his competitors. Dan's business network is also his social network.

Once they establish a relationship, elite providers make every effort to keep nurturing and deepening it. I learned this from someone who was a friend first and later became a client. Every time he sent me an email or talked to me on the phone, he first asked something about my family or something of interest to me away from business.

This was a bit of a revelation to me. I had the view that business was business. If I did a good job, that was enough for a business relationship. However, as I did more research into the elite providers and the importance of relationship in winning the business, I began to pay more attention to the personal side. Now whenever I talk to a client, I try to be proactive and start with the personal. It makes my job more fun, and I win more.

But once you start gathering personal information, you need to remember it so that you don't ask the same personal questions every time you talk. It's a real turnoff when you forgot you previously talked about something personal with a client. I try to keep track of personal information by putting it at the top of my notes in Outlook. That way their personal information is right there in front of me.

Recently, I got a call from a client who I had not spoken to in months. When I brought up his contact information in Outlook and read the notes from our last conversation, where he revealed that his daughter was applying to colleges, we were able to pick up the conversation right where we left off.

"The best time to sell is when they are not buying"

Jeff Colton, a vice president and branch manager for ValleyCrest Landscape Development, doesn't wait for the transaction to build relationships. By then it may be too late. He says he does some of his best selling when clients aren't buying. When clients are in the middle of a deal, everybody wants to see them so it's hard to get any quality time. On the other hand clients are far more accessible between deals. Jeff says that is the best time to build personal and professional relationships.

A designer told me how she lost a recent project for a client who seemed to love her previous work. As it turns out, she had not seen the client since the previous project was finished five years earlier. That's why she lost.

Accelerating personal relationships is not just something to do externally to win new clients. It will also accelerate your success within your company. Most service providers spend as much time selling internally as they do externally. If you are a lender, how much time do you spend trying to convince underwriting to accept your deals? Who do you think has the advantage when the manager hands out promotions?

Fake Sincerity

As you read this, you may be thinking that this all sounds a bit manipulative. In the wrong hands it could be. There is an old saying that the key to success is sincerity. Once you can fake that, everything else is easy. But most people can't affect sincerity. If you attempt to build relationships without being sincerely interested, it shows, and your attempts will backfire. I would suggest that you adjust your attitude before you attempt to find common ground because most clients can read the non-verbal queues. If the client perceives you to be insincere, you will do more harm than good.

Accelerating your personal relationships is the single most effective way to win more business in competition, create highly satisfied clients, gain leverage in negotiations, and advance your career. Therefore, it should not be left to chance or done in an ad hoc manner. Waiting until you see pictures on the wall or trophies on the desk doesn't cut it. You want to be proactive and systematic. Find and deepen common ground with every contact and colleague, and do it with sincerity. You will not only win more business, you will enjoy your work more and your clients will be more committed and loyal.

DELIBERATE PRACTICE FOR ACCELERATING RELATIONSHIPS

Accelerating a personal relationship is the easiest yet most powerful way to build preference, but you still have to practice it to build mastery. You are welcome to use my four relationship acceleration questions:

1. How long have you been in this position?
2. What did you do before?
3. Did you grow up and do your schooling here?
4. Do you live in the area?

Or write three or four of your own. Now begin practicing these questions with anyone. Play the Relationship (Battleship) Game. It can be at a cocktail party, with an existing client, or with a new potential client. Keep working on it until it becomes second nature. See if you can't uncover an "amazing story" with every new person you meet. You'll be surprised how much you have in common with most people. By systematically and proactively searching for common ground, you will find that your job gets easier and more fun.

Develop a tracking system where personal information is kept and easily accessible.

Chapter 5

Accelerating Professional Relationships

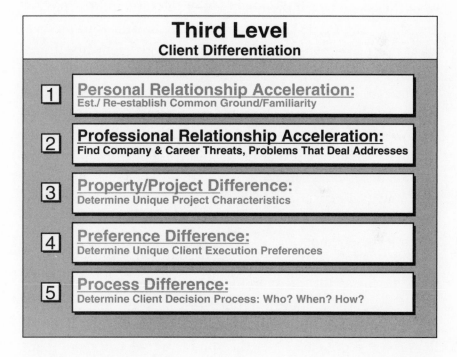

Third Level
Client Differentiation

1. **Personal Relationship Acceleration:**
Est./ Re-establish Common Ground/Familiarity

2. **Professional Relationship Acceleration:**
Find Company & Career Threats, Problems That Deal Addresses

3. **Property/Project Difference:**
Determine Unique Project Characteristics

4. **Preference Difference:**
Determine Unique Client Execution Preferences

5. **Process Difference:**
Determine Client Decision Process: Who? When? How?

Figure 5.1 Who Understands the Client's Business and Role Better?

While the first driver of choice is based upon personal relationship, the second driver is your professional knowledge of the
client—do you, the provider, know this client better professionally? If you are going to be their partner, clients want you to understand their business, market, situation, threats, and objectives.

The more you know about them the more it builds confidence that you will take care of *it* and *them* better than those other vendors.

"WE RESEARCH THE HELL OUT OF THEM"

As the due date for the proposal presentation nears, most companies assemble members of their team in a meeting room to discuss what they want to tell the client about the firm and the project and then assign roles and responsibilities to write and present. The same players will end up saying pretty much the same things they always say in these client presentations.

Instead, direct your team to focus on the client. Try to find out as much as possible about the prospective client's business. As one of my clients put it, "We research the hell out of them. We do web searches, review publications and financials. We look for executives or board members that we know or call people we know who may know them. We want to know their business issues, competition, and objectives. We weave that information into our presentations."

Your value is in the problems you solve better than competitors. The bigger the client problem, the greater your value if you can help. Solve a strategic problem—a problem that threatens their company or their career—and you will be more valuable than if you simply solve a tactical problem, one that helps them do their job a little faster, better, or cheaper.

Let me give you an example of how strategic information led to an unlikely win for Grubb & Ellis. Shawn Mobley, who runs the Chicago office for Grubb & Ellis, received an RFP for an office building disposition from a client with whom they had never worked. Shawn knew that the likelihood of winning an unsolicited RFP was remote.

Before deciding whether to respond, his team did a little research on the company and discovered a presentation that the client CEO had recently made to investors about a new strategy the firm was pursuing that would require it to make major changes to its facilities. This realignment would require not just disposition support as contemplated in the RFP, but a whole range of real estate services. Because Grubb & Ellis offers that full range of services, Shawn and his team decided to respond not just to this one sale but to the whole strategic need.

The client's first reaction to the proposal was concern that Grubb & Ellis had somehow uncovered company secrets. When it was explained that the information was from public sources, the client was so impressed that Grubb & Ellis was chosen to be their strategic partner for all of their real estate needs going forward.

RAISE THE FLASHLIGHT

Another way to build a strategic partnership is with your questioning strategy. Unfortunately, most providers permanently define themselves as vendors in the eyes of potential clients with their first questions. Usually their first question is too tactical;

- "When is your lease up?"
- "How do you finance your real estate?"
- "What designer did your last project?"
- "Have you thought about selling your property?"

Or worse, they don't ask questions at all and just offer a vendor-centric pitch.

Asking a tactical question is like holding a flashlight too close to the desk. You can only see what is right below the small beam

Figure 5.2 Tactical Questions Hold the Flashlight Too Low.

of light. As you raise the flashlight, you can see more of the desk. One of the best ways to "raise the flashlight" is to ask good strategic questions—ones that uncover threats but do not offend a new client.

What's Your Problem?

Remember the objective. You want to find and align to strategic problems. Those are threats to your client's company or his/her career. Unfortunately questions like "What is your biggest problem?" or the more popular version, "What keeps you awake at night?" are not appropriate for a first meeting and may actually alienate the client. How would you feel if you just met someone and they were asking you what your problems were? You may be thinking, "Who are you? Dr. Phil? Get out of here."

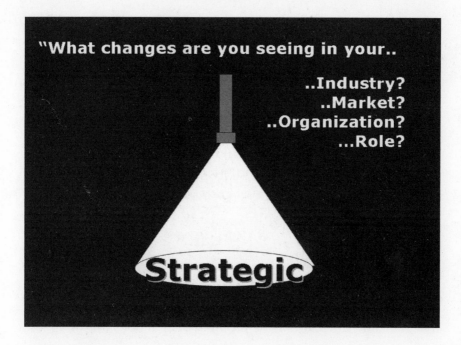

Figure 5.3 Strategic Questions Raise the Flashlight.

WHAT'S CHANGED? THE ULTIMATE
STRATEGIC QUESTION

If you want a non-threatening way to find career and company threats, ask clients about changes to their industry, market, investment strategy, company, or role. Career and company threats are caused when business plans, investments, and objectives meet the reality of a continuously changing market. Changing conditions such as new information, new competitors, changes in demand, regulations, interest rates, technology advances, or legal challenges throw existing plans and methods out of sync, threatening the success of the organization and the career of your client.

What changes have occurred in your prospective client's company or market? What obstacles have those changes created that threaten client performance and personal objectives? Nine times out of 10 when you ask clients about changes they will reveal a problem that threatens their organization or their career. Client problems are the seeds of value for your services. If the client has no problems, your services have no value. On the other hand if you can help the client with strategic problems, you are at your highest value. And even if you can't help with a strategic problem, your knowledge of the client's strategic issues better positions you as a partner instead of a vendor.

LOOKING FOR CID

Once the client reveals a strategic problem, even if it is a problem that you can't solve, probe the problem deeper by asking about the cause, impact, and what they are doing or considering doing about the problem (see Figure 5.4). I call this questioning technique Looking For CID (Cause, Impact, Done, Doing, Considering).

Strategic Partnering

1. **Problem Questions (Value)**
   (Changes?, Challenges?: Industry Market, Company, Role)

2. **Probe Problems for CID:**
   • Cause? (Can you help?)
   • Impact? (Criticality & Urgency?)
   • Done/Doing/Considering? (Resistance?)

Figure 5.4 Looking for CID.

Cause? What caused those problems and obstacles? Asking about the cause lets you know if it is a problem that you can address. Let's say you were a personal trainer, and a potential client mentioned that they had been putting on weight lately. Your first inclination would be to explain your capabilities and offer your services. Instead, you decided to probe more deeply and ask about the cause of the weight gain, and the potential client says that the weight gain was caused by taking steroids for a thyroid condition. Good thing you asked or you would have offered a premature and valueless solution—a common mistake made by vendors.

Impact? The next thing you want to know is how critical and urgent the problem is. Is it one for which this client is going to take action? We all have hundreds of problems, but we will only act on a few. How is the problem impacting the client? What will happen if these obstacles are not addressed? Impact lets you know if this client is motivated to address the problem or objective. By asking about impact, you not only surface criticality and urgency, you are helping the client to think through the cost of not acting on this strategic problem.

Done, Doing, Considering? What have they done, are they doing, or considering doing to address this strategic problem? If the problem is critical and urgent, chances are the client has already done something, is doing something, or is considering doing something. By asking you can uncover potential resistance, something you certainly want to know before you make a recommendation. Perhaps the client tried your solution before and it did not work. Perhaps they are already working with a competitor or are exploring other ways to deal with the problem. Maybe this person simply doesn't have the authority to act. Don't you want to know that before you make any recommendations?

GIVE-AND-TAKE QUESTIONS

Asking questions whose answers are widely available is a good way to put off a potential client. Partners don't ask questions about topics that are covered on the client's web site. Do your research before the meeting. What changes are occurring in the client's industry or market? Have there been changes among their competitors or market share? Look at the public relations page on the client's web site. Check for recent news releases, financial announcements, or reassignments.

Armed with quality research on the prospect, elite business developers use what I call give-and-take questions to initiate a strategic discussion with potential clients. A give-and-take question is a two-step question that first offers information or insight about the prospect's company, industry, market, or competition (give) and then asks the client to share information (take).

By using the give-and-take questioning technique in combination with your change questions, you establish your credibility by sharing your knowledge and insights in exchange for your prospect's comments about his or her strategic situation.

Here are a couple of examples of give-and-take questions:

- The article in *The Wall Street Journal* said you were looking to Asia for 20 percent of your growth next year. How will that change your distribution strategy in the United States?
- Our research indicates that construction material costs have doubled in the last six months. How has that changed your tenant improvement budget?
- Vacancy rates have narrowed in your area. What changes are you seeing?

Some service providers use a more formal give-and-take approach. For example, lenders will frequently arrive armed with a financing strategy "pitch" to create credibility and interest. The key is to keep it interactive. As one banker told me, "If I am going to pitch a variable rate financing, I want to know about the client's previous experience with them before I bring it out. If I find out that they were burned, I'll keep my recommendation in my pocket."

The give-and-take technique is particularly useful for potential clients who are initially reluctant to share their problems and want you to show your hand first. Prospect reluctance (or your preoccupation with your pitch) may force you into a premature and vendor-centric presentation of your capabilities or ideas. Try not to fall into this trap. Whenever possible, turn the presentation back into an exchange.

If you are more familiar with the client, you can then use the more direct problem questions. To keep it strategic ask about objectives first and then ask about challenges. As I write this, it's January and most of my clients are wrapping up the last year and planning for the coming year. This is a particularly good time to explore last year's problems and next year's objectives. Once you uncover a problem, look for CID.

GAINING AGREEMENT TO EXPLORE SOLUTIONS

If their strategic problem is one that you can support, gain agreement to explore your solutions using the following steps:

- Summarize client problems where you can help. "You mentioned that off shoring was reducing your need for office space in Chicago leaving you with expensive unused space."
- Convert problem to an objective and then verify the objective. "So your objective is to right size your space needs and reduce your costs. Is that right?"

Strategic Partnering

1. Problem Questions (Value)
   (Give & Take Changes?)

2. Probe Problems for CID:
   • Cause? (Can you help?)
   • Impact? (Criticality & Urgency?)
   • Done/Doing/Considering? (Resistance?)

3. Gaining Agreement to Explore Solutions
   • Feedback & Convert to and Verify Objective
   • "Would you be interested in exploring..."

Figure 5.5 Give-and-Take Questions to Start Strategic Discussion.

• Gain agreement to explore your solutions. "Would you be interested in exploring ways to better match your space needs and budget to your changing market conditions?" (See Figure 5.5)

Ready, Fire, Aim

Offering solutions before you fully understand and are aligned to the client is a bit like shooting a shotgun in the air and hoping a duck will fly over. Shooting off unaligned solutions is a great way to permanently define yourself as a vendor. If you want to establish a partnership, aim before you shoot, and make sure the client is ready to move with you. Get permission to explore a solution. When you get permission, you will still want to know more about the project, this client's preferences, and the decision process before offering your recommendation. But we are getting ahead of ourselves.

In summary, clients want to work with partners who understand their business. Use your research and questioning strategy to build your knowledge of the threats faced by your clients, even those not related to your services. Start with informed give-and-take questions about changes and challenges. Explore each problem deeper by looking for CID—cause, impact, done, doing and considering. If you uncover something that you can support, convert it to an objective and then gain agreement to explore solutions. You will not only be viewed more as a partner, but also you will likely uncover bigger assignments in the process.

Even after you uncover problems and gain agreement to explore solutions, hold your fire. You still are not ready to offer a solution. You need the other client differentiators before you can align your recommendation. We will show you how top producers do that in the next few chapters.

DELIBERATE PRACTICE TO ACCELERATE PROFESSIONAL RELATIONSHIPS

At the end of the day the conversation techniques presented here are just good communications. You are simply focusing the conversation on them and not you—client-centric versus vendor-centric. Mastering this partnership questioning strategy will take more deliberate practice than any other skill in this book. You can practice with anyone: a friend, a spouse, someone you have just met, or a client. You will be surprised how quickly the conversation deepens. The more interest you show in them the more interest they will have in you.

(Continued)

1. Start by asking about changes: *What is changing at work?*
2. When a problem is raised, any problem, explore it for CID.
   - Cause: What caused that? Why did that happen?
   - Impact: How is that impacting you? What does that mean to you?
   - Done, doing, considering: What are you doing about it? What are you thinking about doing?

When you feel comfortable with the strategic questioning strategy in a non-threatening environment, try it with a new potential client. If their strategic problem is one that you can support, summarize the problem, convert it to an objective, and then gain agreement to explore a solution.

- Feedback and verify objective: *You mentioned that competition has reduced your margins and limited your cash on hand, so your objective is to generate more cash, is that right?*
- *Would you be interested in exploring ways to better leverage your real estate to raise cash?*

Once again your attitude is more important than the technique. Be interested in their business issues, and the questions will come naturally.

Chapter 6

Finding Project/Property Difference

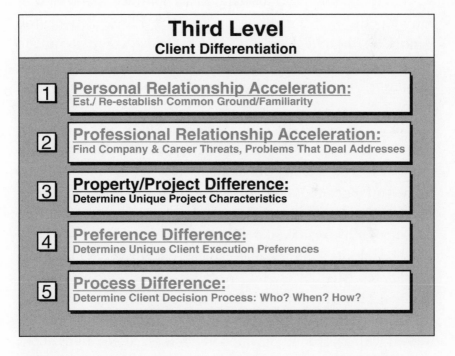

Third Level
Client Differentiation

1. **Personal Relationship Acceleration:**
   Est./ Re-establish Common Ground/Familiarity

2. **Professional Relationship Acceleration:**
   Find Company & Career Threats, Problems That Deal Addresses

3. **Property/Project Difference:**
   Determine Unique Project Characteristics

4. **Preference Difference:**
   Determine Unique Client Execution Preferences

5. **Process Difference:**
   Determine Client Decision Process: Who? When? How?

Figure 6.1 What is Different About the Project, Property or Market?

Most client interactions occur in the context of an actual transaction. To clients, top service providers look alike, but they view their own project as completely unique. In addition to your personal and professional relationship acceleration, if you can find and align to those unique project and property differences, then you can more effectively separate yourself from competitors.

Unlike other investments, like stocks and bonds, every property is different. Its location, improvements, use, positioning, fixtures, floor plan, tenant mix, and multiple other characteristics make each one different from the next. Yet most of the real estate research attempts to bundle properties and compare them to "comparable" properties in order to value them.

Vendor-centric providers tend to accept this generic view of the property when executing transactions. Elite, client-centric partners, on the other hand, find out what makes a property unique and then leverage that information for the benefit of their client. As a result, they win more business and create more value for their clients.

Recall my story about the three landscape architects. The first two architects took a vendor-centric approach. They spent our time together talking about themselves and their capabilities. Their working assumption was that the more we knew about them, the more likely we would be to choose them. To them we were just another backyard and pool.

By contrast, the third landscape architect was client-centric. He differentiated *on us*. But in doing so, he went beyond the personal. He didn't simply try to get to know us or establish rapport. Instead of presenting his brochure, as the first two had done, he walked with us around our property and asked questions about the unique characteristic of our yard.

One of the first things he saw was the large willow tree that dominated the yard. Were we aware, he asked, that its leaves would be a maintenance problem for our dreamed-of swimming pool, and that its roots would probably damage the pool within a few years?

We talked about the contours of our property. When he told me about some drainage easements that are written into our title, it emerged that we would have to put the pool in a different place from what my wife and I had anticipated—willow tree or no willow tree. We also learned that putting a cover on the pool would dictate its shape.

To the vendor-centric providers, we represented another backyard, another pool, hardscape, and softscape. By talking about themselves, they tried to match *our* project to *their* capabilities. They completely missed the drainage easement problem.

The client-centric provider focused on what was distinctive about our property and project. By doing so, he demonstrated his capabilities and his competence. He also inspired in us a sense of commitment and trust.

Project or property alignment is every bit as important and effective when the stakes are higher than a backyard landscape project. In fact, the bigger the numbers, the greater the scope or complexity of the project, the more critically important it is to differentiate on the client, not yourself.

Colliers International won a much larger engagement by finding and aligning to what was unique about the project and the properties involved. Just as the numbers were bigger, the project was more complex. But the basic process of aligning with the project was the same. It just took more work and more resources.

Recall the Standard Life Investments choice we used in Chapter 2 as an example of how clients choose among alternatives. Traditionally, the company had handled the leasing and management of its real estate holdings. But, after successfully outsourcing commercial real estate services in some European countries, Standard Life decided that managing its own properties was not a core competency. So the company began a search for a partner to take over those duties for its portfolio of Canadian properties.

In typical fashion, Standard Life sent requests for information (RFI) to 10 vendors, then screened the competitors for a short list of three preferred providers, including Colliers. The three were asked to respond to and then present their proposal response in 15 days.

There were 69 different properties involved in the project. But George Chambers, the Colliers senior vice president in charge of the proposal, was determined to differentiate on Standard Life and its properties. So he directed the Colliers property management and brokerage teams across Canada to visit every one of the 69 properties in person, photograph it, and provide a detailed assessment of each.

The two other short-listed providers offered a classic vendor-centric presentations—here's who we are, what we do, who we've done it for, and what we can do for you.

The Colliers presentation was different. It featured a 15-page SWOT (strength, weakness, opportunity, threat) analysis of the 69 properties. A photo of each one captured not just its appearance but the local weather as well. Alongside each photo was a concise assessment of current tenants, traffic access and parking, and competitive issues and opportunities in the local commercial market.

In short, the Colliers proposal was a comprehensive report on Standard Life's Canadian assets and how Colliers would manage each property going forward. Not surprisingly, the presentation quickly turned into a dialogue between the Colliers people and the Standard Life decision makers—a discussion that went well beyond the two hours allotted. Within a few days, Colliers was awarded the portfolio, worth more than $350 million.

According to Peter Cuthbert, vice-president of SLIRE and the person responsible for coordinating the client decision, Colliers had initially been the dark horse in the competition. But Colliers demonstrated a higher commitment and deeper understanding of the properties. That gave him comfort that the Colliers professionals understood what they were getting into and would make the best partner.

Of course, much went into the Colliers' pitch for this handsome piece of business. George Chambers is a seasoned practitioner of Third-Level Selling, and he orchestrated a masterful effort. He made sure to accelerate the personal and professional relationships between his team and the decision makers at Standard Life. He took care to understand their preferences and processes, and he aligned the Colliers' proposal accordingly.

But the SWOT analysis, which aligned Colliers with the essence of the project—the 69 properties to be managed—was probably the masterstroke. After the contract was awarded, the Standard Life people told Colliers that their pitch and their proposal had been superior at every stage of the process, from the RFI stage through the RFP and the final presentation. But what the Standard Life people said they were most impressed with was the time, effort, and care that went into visiting and assessing each property.

"OUR BROKERS NEED TO KNOW OUR BUILDINGS BETTER THAN WE DO"

Lori Johanson is a senior vice president with Citi Realty Services' Global Capital Transactions, a small group of professionals at Citigroup that is responsible for consulting on the company's large real estate transactions. Lori's task is particularly challenging because her team has so many locations and constituents. In the last two years alone, Lori has been part of the interview process to select firms to represent them on deals in San Francisco, Dallas, Chicago, Atlanta, Miami, and Puerto Rico ranging from 250,000 to 1.5 million square feet. They have to serve stockholders, senior managers, and a variety of users from high-end investment bankers at Smith Barney to back office support staff.

It would be impossible to keep up with all of these markets, buildings, owners, and users. That is why, according to Johanson, "Our brokers need to know our buildings better than we do." So when brokers pitch a generic approach, it is a pretty good indicator that they are not potential partners in the transaction.

"BECAUSE YOU DIDN'T ASK"

The Colliers story is a study in bold, proactive project/property alignment. But project alignment happens or not, and pays off or not, at the most fundamental level as well. And there are no excuses for not being proactive.

A rep for one of my clients, a commercial landscape architecture firm, once told me a classic story of how he lost a substantial piece of business by failing to align with the project. When he received an RFP from a retail mall client, the RFP said nothing about timing, so he presented a proposal based on a normal timeline for the scope of the project in question.

When his firm didn't win the business, the rep asked the client why. "Because your timeline for the project was too long," the client replied, and he went on to explain that he needed the project completed before the holidays. Otherwise, his tenants would suffer from reduced traffic and sales during the biggest selling season of the year, and he'd be on the hook for their losses.

Somewhat taken aback, the rep asked the client why he hadn't told him about the timing issue before. The client said, "Because you didn't ask. The other firm did."

You can never assume that RFPs will tell you everything you need to know about a project. Indeed, they may just leave out the most important details—the ones you can use to build preference for your proposal. That's why the deliberate practice at the end of this chapter is to develop and put to use a strategy for discovering and tracking the differentiators you can use to align with every project and property.

What questions would you ask to uncover unique project characteristics? Start with strategic questions and then work your way to more tactical issues.

- How does this project fit into your overall strategy? Why this project? Why now?
- What is unique about the project that could affect value, timing, design, underwriting, improvements, tenant mix, retention, value, work load, disruption, image, traffic, access, usage, resale, and so on?

START THE PROJECT BEFORE THE MANDATE

Instead of telling the potential client what you are going to do, give a preview of what a working relationship with you feels like. Actually start the project. Doing that adds risk and effort, but it gives both you and the client a head start.

That's how Bob Hess, a consulting partner with Cushman & Wakefield, wins competitive business. Bob helps companies locate and evaluate properties to execute their business strategy.

When ThyssenKrupp, a Fortune 1000 German steel conglomerate was looking to expand operations in China, they needed a location adviser for their $1 billion capital investment. Hess' competitors tried to persuade ThyssenKrupp to hire them based upon their experience and local capabilities; Bob took the risk of actually starting the project before the client chose a provider.

He and his team invested more than 80 hours of background research and a trip to Shanghai on spec to further clarify project needs and to conduct empirical research into the local joint venture, the industry, and local site selection issues the company would face expanding as a wholly owned subsidiary in this new market.

When it came time to make final presentations in Germany, Hess' competitors presented their capabilities and experience (vendor-centric). Hess' team presented what they had learned about the client and the project (client-centric).

By starting the project before the mandate, they demonstrated commitment in addition to project knowledge. Instead of a promise to do something in the future, Hess' team offered a more certain outcome with proven results. That built client confidence, and Hess' team realized significant fees for what turned out to be a comparatively small upfront investment.

RFP's ask you about qualifications, approach, and costs, but they frequently don't go into detail about the unique aspects of the project or property. But it is in those unique aspects that you can build differentiation. If you are the only one who knows about them, you have a huge advantage. Since you are going to find out about them anyway when and if you are awarded the business, why not find out about them earlier to improve your chances of winning?

DELIBERATE PRACTICE: PROJECT/PROPERTY DIFFERENTIATION

This should be the easiest of the transfer exercises because you probably do a good job of differentiating on the project/property now. All I want to do here is change the timing.

What is the first thing you do when you are awarded a deal? You probably attempt to find out as much as you can about the project. What is unique about it that could affect pricing, underwriting, image, timing, leasing, designing, and so on? But why wait until after you are awarded the deal. Find and align to the differences before the award so that you are more likely to win it in the first place.

First, find out about the strategic fit of the property/project.

- Why this project at this time?
- How does it fit into the overall strategy of the firm?
- What is unique about the property that could threaten or accelerate the outcome?

Use this information to build your presentations and recommendations.

Chapter 7

Finding and Aligning to Client Preferences

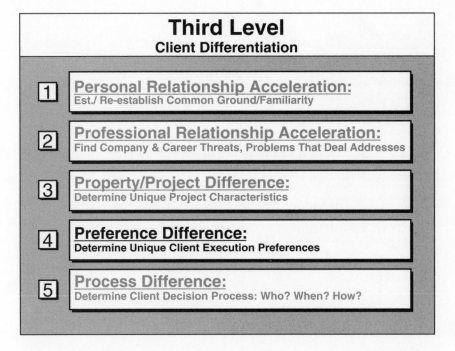

Third Level
Client Differentiation

1. **Personal Relationship Acceleration:**
   Est./ Re-establish Common Ground/Familiarity

2. **Professional Relationship Acceleration:**
   Find Company & Career Threats, Problems That Deal Addresses

3. **Property/Project Difference:**
   Determine Unique Project Characteristics

4. **Preference Difference:**
   Determine Unique Client Execution Preferences

5. **Process Difference:**
   Determine Client Decision Process: Who? When? How?

Figure 7.1 What Unique Preferences Does Each Decision Maker Bring to This Decision?

As we presented in the previous chapter, you want to find and align to what is unique about the property or project. But you will also want to find what is unique about each client decision maker and influencer. Where project differences attach to the property, preferences attach to the decision maker.

Each client brings a unique bias, history, understanding, alternatives, concern, knowledge, and vision to a service provider decision. These factors drive their preferences when choosing among competitors. As we discussed earlier, clients all want to achieve the best outcome. That usually means they want the best price with the least:

- Risk
- Effort
- Disruption
- Surprises
- Time
- Cost

If you can find and align to each decision maker's and influencer's preferences, clients will choose you more often. Client preferences emerge from four areas:

1. Previous experience (usually bad)
2. Current execution concerns
3. Client's vision of the best outcome and best approach
4. Competition

PREVIOUS EXPERIENCE

Previous experiences with service providers, particularly bad experiences, often are the biggest drivers of client preference. As the old saying goes, we learn most from our mistakes. If a client made a mistake in a past decision, they will bring that lesson to future decisions.

For example, if a client was retraded at the 11th hour in their last transaction, you can be sure they will try to work with a broker who will avoid that this time. If they chose the low-bid contractor and then faced continuous and expensive change orders, next time they will look for a contractor who will offer more budget certainty, even if their initial bid is higher. If they had to do more work than they expected, they will look for a provider who will minimize their effort. If they had trouble reaching the provider during critical points, they will look for a more responsive partner.

Lenders frequently have the hardest time creating difference in preference in the mind of clients. After all each lender's money is just as green as their competitor's money, so it is not uncommon for lenders to assume that clients only make decisions based on rate and terms. But in my interviews with clients, price (within a range), is not the only decision influencer even when borrowing money.

If the terms and conditions were substantially changed at the last minute in a previous financing, or the documentation was burdensome, took too much time, or involved too much in legal bills, that client won't make the next decision based on a few basis points difference in rates. Don't get me wrong, pricing must be competitive, but within a client's price range, price is still the last of the 10 differentiators.

EDUCATING CLIENT CONCERNS

Experienced service buyers know what to worry about. Each project brings its own distinct problems that concern clients. You will want to uncover both their general concerns about execution as well as their specific concerns about this particular project.

A less-experienced client may not even be aware of the threats to a deal's execution, so your ability to mitigate that risk won't be valued. Investors who are in and out of the market frequently generally have clearly defined preferences and decision criteria. But for many clients this project may be the first and only time that they're faced with these decisions. For example, a lease may only come up once every five to 10 years. By the time the next tenant improvement occurs, this office manager or facilities manager may be retired.

Clients who are infrequently in the market may need to be educated about the execution risks before they can understand the value of your differences. Let me give you another example again from my backyard. This time I needed a little education in order to have a preference.

One of the areas where I felt most comfortable going with the lowest bidder was the stonework. With 1,200 square feet of Connecticut Bluestone to put down, I saw this as an area to save money. Once again I identified three contractors through references and asked each to give us a bid. One of the bids was considerably higher than the other two. I told the contractor with the highest price that he might want to sharpen his pencil if he wanted to be considered.

He asked me if I'd ever had stonework done before. When I told him that I had not, he started asking questions that caused me to reconsider my low-bid strategy. He asked if the other contractors were going to lay out the stone before they set it. I said I didn't know and asked why that was important. He said that Connecticut Bluestone came in lots of different colors from blue to gray to rust to red. If the contractor did not lay out the stone first to see the color spread, it could lead to color blotching. I did not know that.

He continued by asking if the other contractors were going to lay out the stone in order to see that there would be no short edges. Once again I did not know the answer and asked why that was important. He said that it was unlikely that the stone would be a perfect fit in the space where it was going to be installed, and you wanted to avoid having an edge with only one or two inches of stone.

Finally he asked me whether the other contractors were going to "butter" the bottom of each stone before laying it down so that it would create an air seal. He explained that the air seal would keep the stone from popping up in future years.

As I learned more, my concern grew, and as my concern grew, my decision moved further and further from price. Once I was educated as to all the risks of the stonework, I decided it might be safer to choose the more expensive contractor.

WHAT COULD GO WRONG?

In Chapter 3 I suggested that you map out the execution process in order to build your positioning statement. Now I suggest that you review that process map and then develop a questioning strategy to help the client see those execution risks so that your positioning creates value.

What were your differences? In what areas are you able to get a better outcome with less risk, effort, time, and fewer surprises than your best competitors? What questions could you ask a client that would raise their concern about unforeseen execution issues?

Notice that the higher-priced stone contractor did not just list his advantages. Instead he asked me questions so I would think about the impact of certain differences in execution. He did not just tell me that he laid out the stones and buttered the back, he asked me about the impact of color blotching, poorly measured end pieces, and popping stonework. That caused me to think more about the problem and what it would mean to me.

Don't just present your advantages to the client, develop a questioning strategy that uncovers the impact. For example, instead of just saying that the schedule could slip if something's not done, ask the client about how important it is to meet the time schedule, or even better, ask the client what the impact would be if it is not completed on time.

Once the client has been educated to the execution issue, your ability to mitigate those issues becomes more valuable. Additionally, your raising the concern is a good way to communicate your expertise. Remember the third landscape architect never showed me his brochure or said that he was more experienced. He didn't have to. I could tell from his questions that he was very knowledgeable.

CLIENT VISIONS

As we've said before, when you sell a service, you're selling something that doesn't exist. It's a promise to do something in the future. And in most cases you need the active support and participation of the client to ensure a successful outcome. In fact the client is a co-manufacturer of the outcome. You and your clients form a partnership to successfully execute the project.

Clients often feel that if they had the time, they could execute this project as well or better than anyone. After all they know their property and this project better than anyone else, and they may have been through the process many times before. If you can find and align to that vision, once again you have an opportunity to create preference in the mind of this client. Here are a few questions to surface client visions:

- What are your (the client's) expectations for this project?
- What do you consider the best approach to be? Why?
- What outcome are you expecting? Why?
- How is this project similar or different from your previous projects? How should those differences affect outcome and approach?

Sometimes service providers don't want to know the answers to these questions because it forces them to approach the deal in a different way or because they feel they know more than the client does. But if you view your client as your partner, either take guidance from their knowledge and skills or educate them as to why your approach may be better to achieve their objective. Acquiring and reconciling client expectations early is the best way to avoid problems later. The longer you wait to solve a problem, the harder and more expensive it is to fix.

YOUR COMPETITION

The safest way for clients to ensure a good decision, particularly for decisions where the client doesn't have experience, is to leverage market forces. When I have to buy a product or service that I don't know very much about, I let competition be my teacher. Competitors will let me know what the key issues are and what characteristics or approaches are better. In addition each competitor will bring a unique approach that others have not considered. These become part of the client's visions.

I'm always amazed when service providers don't explore who their competition is, what the client's current perception of the competition is, and what new ideas the competitors are offering.

When I question providers about not asking about competition, they explain that clients may not want to disclose who they are competing against. In my experience if a client doesn't want to tell you who you are competing against, it is because you are not the preferred provider. The preferred provider gets the inside information because the client wants them to win.

Coaches explore their competitor's strengths and weaknesses exhaustively in order to position their strengths against competitor weaknesses. Don't you have different advantages when compared to different competitors? Consider using the following questions to uncover competitive information to position against:

- Who else has been invited to compete for your business?
- Have you worked with any of them before?
- (If so) What went well?
- What could have been done better? (Notice here I am going back to previous experience. If something didn't go well the last time, this gives me the best opportunity to position against that provider.) Don't just leave it there, explore it for CID:
  - What caused that?
  - How did that impact you?
  - What did you do about it or what are you thinking this time around to avoid that?
- What do you see as the relative strengths and weaknesses of the service providers you've invited?
- Have you heard any ideas that sound attractive to you?
- What will be your criteria for choosing a provider?
- How will you compare and measure that?

Let me give you an example of finding and aligning to unique client preferences. The CEO of a commercial construction company asked me to help his team win a multi-million-dollar assignment for tenant improvements to the San Francisco offices of a financial services company.

I started by reviewing the construction company's proposal. Classically vendor-centric, it was almost entirely about the contractor's company: when they were founded, how many offices they had, their corporate values, what projects they had done and for whom, and so forth. By now you should be able to recognize what was missing from this proposal. There was virtually nothing about this client or this project in the proposal beyond what was provided in the RFP.

Another contractor in the competition had performed services for the client before. I advised my contractor client that unless his team could differentiate their proposal on the client, they would almost certainly lose unless they "bought" the business with a low bid. With that in mind, my client and his team went back to interview the project manager for the financial services firm.

My contractor client discovered that the project manager (his prospective client) of this rapidly growing financial services company was concerned that she was being stretched too thin with multiple building projects in multiple cities occurring simultaneously. She felt that she needed to "walk the site" daily to stay on top of things, but she would not be able to do that with four projects going on at the same time.

With this new client preference information, my commercial contractor client changed his proposal to include a web-based dashboard where his superintendent would post pictures and updates on a daily basis so that the project manager could "walk the site" virtually whenever and wherever she wanted. The project manager was so delighted with the creative solution that she awarded that contractor the three remaining projects without a competitive bid.

UNHOOKING AN INCUMBENT COMPETITOR

If the client has no problem with their current provider, it is almost impossible for you to create preference and unhook the incumbent. So, if the client is already using one of your competitors, you have to find chinks in the armor to establish a beachhead of value.

Start by asking the client what is working well with their current vendor. If you start by asking about problems, the client may feel the need to defend the incumbent since they may have picked them in the first place. In my experience, when you ask what is going well, clients will frequently go directly to what is not going well anyway. Try it. Next ask them what areas they would like to see improved.

If they do share a problem, probe it as much as possible to focus the client's attention on the issue and to establish a platform for your own differentiators. Again look for CID—ask about the cause of the problem, the impact the problem is having on the client, and what the client is considering as alternatives before you offer yourself as a solution.

Preference Difference

Execution *Preferences:*
- ❑ **Previous Experiences**
  - ❑ **Tell me about previous projects?**
  - ❑ **Who did it? What went well? What didn't?**
  - ❑ **What caused that? How did that impact you?**
- ❑ **Client Execution Concerns**
  - ❑ **What are your concerns about risk, effort, timing**
- ❑ **Client's Current Vision for Outcome and Approach**
  - ❑ **What is the best way to approach this?**
  - ❑ **What are you looking for? Criteria?**
- ❑ **Competition**
  - ❑ **Who else is invited?**
  - ❑ **How would you compare us now?**
  - ❑ **What alternative approaches look attractive?**
  - ❑ **Why?**

Figure 7.2 Look for Concerns to Build a Platform for Your Differentiators.

DELIBERATE PRACTICE: FINDING DIFFERENCES IN CLIENT PREFERENCES

Think about the things that could go wrong for the client that would:

- Change the outcome
- Increase the risk
- Increase client effort/workload
- Increase surprises/disruption
- Slow the process
- Add to hidden costs
- Other problems

Which of these are or should be most important to clients? What questions would you ask to build awareness of the cause and impact of these? Interview a potential client. Uncover their unique preferences using the following questions:

Client's Previous Experiences

- Tell me about previous projects?
- Who did it? What went well? What didn't?
- What caused that? How did that impact you?

Client's Execution Concerns

- What are your concerns for this project?
- What would be the impact of ... blown budget, missed schedule, and so on.

(Continued)

Client's Current Vision for Outcome and Approach

- What do you think is the best way to approach this?
- How do you see this playing out?

Competition

- Who else is invited?
- How would you compare us now?
- What (criteria) are you looking for?
- What alternative approaches or ideas look attractive? Why?

Each client decision maker or influencer brings unique perspective and preferences to a service provider decision. These can rarely be found in the RFP. You have to go looking for them. They come from previous experiences, current concerns, client expectations and the competition.

Chapter 8

Finding and Aligning to the Client's Decision Process

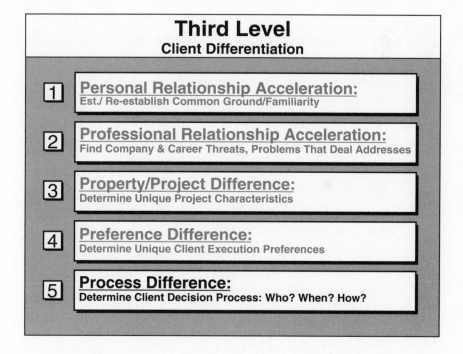

Figure 8.1 Who, When, and How Will They Decide?

Have you ever spent months working with a client only to discover that the person with whom you were dealing did not have the authority to make the decision? High-level real estate transactions frequently have lots of moving parts and layers. They can take months and sometimes years to complete. There is frequently more than one decision maker, influencer, or other stakeholder involved. Finally, the timing of the decision may affect who and why a particular provider is chosen. Finding and aligning to the decision process is the final client differentiator. Let me offer a couple of examples:

A successful partner of a consulting firm that provides location forecasting models invited me to join him in a meeting with the vice president of real estate for a large apparel company. The location consultant did a great job of finding and aligning to his client's strategic issues and exploring them for CID (cause, impact and done, doing, considering), but failed to align to the client's decision process.

After a few personal questions to find common ground, here is how the conversation went:

Location consultant: What *changes* are you seeing in your market?

VP of real estate: It is becoming more challenging to maintain our margins as we accelerate our growth.

Location consultant: What is *causing* that?

VP of real estate: We have saturated the primary markets. Our future growth will come from secondary and tertiary markets. The big markets were easy. It is getting tougher to make good decisions in these smaller markets.

Location consultant: How is that *impacting* you?

VP of real estate: The number of underperforming stores has been increasing. About 10 percent are now underperforming.

Location consultant: What is the difference between an average-performing store and an under-performing store?

VP of real estate: An average-performing store brings in $1 million a year more than the weak performers.

Location consultant: How is that *impacting* you?

VP of real estate: Location mistakes can't be resolved quickly because stores are usually locked into a seven- to ten-year lease. That means that each "mistake" location costs $7 million to $10 million.

Location consultant: So one in ten stores turn out to be poor locations, and each of those are draining $7 million to $10 million from profits over the term of the lease. My guess is that as you move in to secondary markets that percentage may increase.

VP of real estate: That's what I am worried about.

Location consultant: Would you be interested in exploring ways to screen out weak locations before stores were built?

By questioning instead of presenting capabilities, the location consultant was able to find and align to the VP of real estate's strategic issue. It seemed clear that bad locations posed a significant drag on earnings.

At that point the location consultant described how they used lifestyle demographics and other location predictors to preview the performance of a store at a proposed location. According to the location consultant, they were able to reduce location mistakes by 75 percent. The VP of Real Estate was thrilled with the possibilities and invited the location consultant to make a proposal presentation in front of the CFO and CEO.

When the day came to present his proposal, the location consultant felt confident that this prospect would soon be a client. After he was introduced to the CFO and CEO, the location consultant launched into his client-centric proposal presentation.

Location consultant: Steve, (the VP of real estate) you said that your margins are being negatively impacted by under-performing stores whose four-wall contribution is $1 million less per year than your average store. Further, your lease provisions prevent you from mitigating the problem for seven to ten years, leaving you with a $7 million to $10 million loss per store. So your objective is to improve margins by reducing location mistakes.

We can help you improve your margins going forward by significantly reducing the location mistakes before stores are leased and opened. That's because you will be able to more accurately predict sales by location using our profile and forecasting models. Clients who have used these models have reduced location mistakes by 75 percent.

And here is where the trouble began. At this point in the presentation, the CEO turned to the real estate VP and said that as far as he was concerned, the problem with the under-performing stores was not so much the location as it was the weak managers in those stores. To that, the CFO revealed that a consultant she had already retained suggested the problem was with the merchandising. The three executives continued to make their conflicting cases on the *causes* of poor store performance using up most of the presentation time.

What happened? The real estate consultant had done a good job of uncovering the real estate VP's strategic issue and had aligned and presented his proposal presentation to it.

Although the VP of real estate was ready, it is clear that he was not the only decision maker. He was part of a decision-making team that included both the CEO and the CFO. These three executives had not even reached a consensus on the cause of their problem; furthermore, they did not share a common vision or agree on a path toward resolution of the problem. The location consultant was also unaware that a competitor was already working with the CFO.

In a multi-decision-maker environment like the one above, you need to differentiate with *all* of the stakeholders and attempt to create a consensus case. It was now clear that the consulting partner had offered a premature solution. So far, he had differentiated on only one of the stakeholders.

Often, as this example shows, it's not a prospect's willingness to make a decision but the decision process itself that knocks a potential deal off track.

Nothing is worse than spending months with a receptive prospect only to find out that he or she doesn't have the authority or budget to make a decision. Ultimately, the questions you must answer to determine which, if any, action constraints are present in any given situation are:

- Who else will be involved in the decision?
- What will their roles be?
- What are their preferences and criteria?
- Can we meet with them?
- When does the decision need to be made? Why?
- How will the decision be made?

Finding and aligning to the client's unique decision process is the last of the five client differentiators. You are looking for the who, what, when, and why of the service provider decision. Whenever possible, meet with and differentiate on all of the decision makers and influencers.

DELIBERATE PRACTICE: FIND AND ALIGN TO THE DECISION PROCESS

See if you can find out what is unique about your client's decision process. Try asking the following questions:

- When does this need to be completed? Why?
- Who else will be involved?
- What will their roles be?
- Do you know what their preferences are?
- Can I meet (talk) with them?
- Tell me about the decision process?

Chapter 9

Third-Level Proposals and Presentations

FROM VENDOR-CENTRIC TO CLIENT-CENTRIC

The objective of Third-Level Selling is to help you migrate from a vendor to a preferred provider to a strategic partner. Your proposal or presentation is the payoff for all of the deliberate practice you have completed. Now we can combine all of the work you did to accelerate your message in Part I with the work you did to differentiate on the client to build an aligned client-centric proposal and presentation in Part II.

Most proposals and presentations that I see are vendor-centric and generally follow a pattern like this:

- This is who we are (This can include information about people, resources, values, history, etc.)
- This is what we do (Capabilities are the focus of this section and examples of previous successes.)
- This is who we have done for (This usually includes of list of previous clients and perhaps the requisite testimonial letters.)
- Here is what we will do for you (This is the specific response to the RFP specs.)
- Financial considerations and schedule (Pricing information and timeline with roles and responsibilities)

Decision Hierarchy

Client Differentiators: 3rd Level

1. Personal Relationship
2. Professional Relationship
3. Property/Project Difference
4. Preference Difference
5. Process Difference

Vendor Differentiators: 2nd Level

6. Proof
7. Experience
8. Approach
9. Capabilities
10. Price

Figure 9.1 Align Your Differentiators to Your Client's Differentiators to Prepare a Client-Centric Presentation.

THIRD-LEVEL PRESENTATIONS ARE CLIENT-CENTRIC

Third-Level presentations also include capabilities and positioning, but that vendor-centric information is presented in the context of this client's unique client differentiators. Further the focus of a Third-Level presentation is the client not the vendor (see Figure 9.1).

To build partnership you will want to work from a client-centric posture. Partnering means aligning your pitch and positioning to what is unique about each client.

You create maximum preference by aligning your unique service capabilities (vendor differentiators) to the prospective client's unique perception of value (client differentiators). Therefore a

Third Level
Client-centric Presentation

(Client Differentiation)
Property/Project/Preference Difference
1. Client Execution Concerns, Causes, Impact
2. Client Objectives, Timeframes and Constraints
3. Verification: *"Is that correct? What has changed?"*

(Aligned Vendor Differentiation)
Your Aligned Difference
1. Your unique approach/solution
2. Difference: *(How approach is different)*
3. Preference: *(Why difference is important to objective)*
4. Proof: *(Story, benchmark, testimonial)*

Figure 9.2 Third-Level Presentation Flow.

Third-Level presentation shares what you learned that is unique about the client and then aligns what is unique about you to support that client's execution concerns and objectives. Instead of focusing on what is different about you (vendor-centric), build emotional preference by focusing on what is different about the prospective client (client-centric). A Third-Level presentation looks like Figure 9.2.

Dan Winey at the architecture firm Gensler learned early in his career not to present a boilerplate vendor-centric presentation. He and his colleagues were in a bake off for a headquarters remodel for a major publisher in New York. They had prepared 10 boards (this was before PowerPoint) describing Gensler's capabilities, experience, and ideas for the space and were working their way through the presentation when Dan noticed that the client audience seemed distracted.

Sensing that his team was missing the target, Dan gathered up the boards, put them aside, and said to the client, "Guys, let's talk," and began to explore their situation. With that, one by one the members of the client team began to open up about their situation and concerns.

The publishing house had recently merged with another firm, and they were concerned about their loss of identity. They didn't want the standard cubicle design because it didn't reflect the personality of the merged groups. These are issues that one doesn't find in the RFP. Dan discovered that the real issues driving the decision were personal and cultural, not technical.

Dan's team won that business not so much because they were better designers but because they were better listeners. Since those early days, Dan has been on a crusade to eradicate the "I" and "We" from Gensler's proposals and presentations. He wants Gensler's presentations to be an interactive conversation about the client. "Imagine," he says, "how much more interesting it is to the client to see their problem up on the screen rather than your company information."

The previous five chapters offered a map and navigation tools to find client differentiators:

1. Common ground to accelerate personal relationships
2. Strategic threats to client companies and careers to accelerate professional relationships
3. Unique project/property differences
4. Unique client preferences from previous experience, current execution concerns, client visions, and competition
5. Client decision process: Who? How? When?

Third Level™ Client Profile (With Questions)

1. **Personal: Common Ground?**
   Personal Client Info: (Time in position, previous, family, schooling, interests, common ground, etc.)

   - ☐ How long in this position?
   - ☐ What did you do before?
   - ☐ Did you grow up and do your schooling here?
   - ☐ Do you live in the area?

2. **Professional: Strategic and Deal Related Problems?**
   Client Perception of Key Industry, Market, Company, or Internal Changes:

   What changes are you seeing in . . . . .
   - ☐ Industry, market, company, property usage, investment strategy, role?
   - ☐ Tenant retention?
   - ☐ Encroachment by competitors?
   - ☐ Rental rates?

   Key Client Strategic Problems that could threaten career or company:

   When the client shares any problem above, explore it for CID:
   - ☐ Cause?
   - ☐ Impact?
   - ☐ Done, Doing, Considering

   Key Real Estate Problem or Objective You Could Support: How?

   - ☐ What caused you to pursue this project?
     - ○ **CID** – Cause? Impact? What else considered?
   - ☐ Why now?
   - ☐ What are your objectives? What are your constraints?

3. **Project/Property Difference?**
   Unique Project/Property Characteristics that impact risk, price, timing, execution:

   - ☐ What caused you to pursue this project?
     - ○ **CID** – Cause? Impact? What else considered?
   - ☐ Why now?
   - ☐ How does this fit into your overall strategy?
   - ☐ What is unique or unusual about this property?

4. **Preferences Difference?**
   Previous Experience, Concerns, Client's Visions, Competition:

   - ☐ Tell me about previous projects?
   - ☐ Who did it? What went well? What didn't?
   - ☐ What caused that? How did that impact you?
   - ☐ What are your concerns about. . .risk, effort, timing?

☐ What do you think is the best way to approach this?
☐ What are you looking for? Criteria?
☐ Who else is invited?
☐ How would you compare us now?
☐ What alternative approaches look attractive? Why?

5. **Client Decision Process?** (Timing, People, Decision Process?)

☐ Who else will be involved in this decision? What role will they play? What are their criteria? Can we meet with them?
☐ When does this need to be completed? Why?
☐ How will the decision be made?

Your Proof Statement for This Client?: Difference, Preference, Proof?

☐ What can you provably do better than your best competitor to achieve this client's execution objective? Why can you get them a better outcome than anyone else? What is your proof? (Story, benchmark, and testimonial)

Decision Stage and Momentum Recommendation:

☐ What stage? 1. Awareness 2. Assessment 3. Search 4. Evaluation 5. Provider
☐ Recommendation that 1. Fits stage 2. Advances decision 3. Client action
☐ What is best possible outcome? What will you ask the client to do?
☐ What is the least expected outcome? What will you ask the client to do?

Figure 9.3　Client Profile (With Third-level Questions).

Figure 9.3 is a client profile that includes all of my recommended questions to find client differentiation. It is a summary of the map and navigation tools for Third-Level Selling.

Now you can use that unique client information to build a client-centric Third-Level proposal or presentation. Start by feeding back your understanding of the client's situation, concerns, and objectives. Remember it is the client's execution concerns that make your unique approach preferable. So start with the client and then work back to your differentiators that fit the client perception of value. Here is the presentation flow:

1. Feedback Unique Project/Property and Preferences

Review the unique characteristics of the project that could affect the outcome or change the approach. Review client execution concerns, previous good and bad experiences, as well as the client's visions of the best outcome or approach. Take client concerns and convert them to specific objectives and constraints.

2. Verify and Gain Agreement

Before you offer your argument about what you will do and how it is better, verify that your understanding is correct and current. *"Is that correct? Has anything changed?"* This assures that you are still aligned.

There may be new decision makers or influencers present who may have different input. Now is the time to get it even if it drastically changes your presentation. After all you don't want to find out that you were out of alignment after your presentation.

3. Isolate Objectives and Present Difference, Preference, and Proof

What do you offer that is unique, difficult for competitors to duplicate, important to the prospect, and increases the likelihood that the service buyer's objectives will be achieved? Isolate and, whenever possible, name (brand) that capability characteristic. Naming it or giving it a brand further distinguishes this characteristic from alternatives and makes it easier for potential clients to remember.

Instead of taking all of the objectives and answering them together, isolate each one, complete your argument, and gain agreement before proceeding to the next objective. Once you have identified your differentiators and assembled your proof, try scripting your presentation using the following language I introduced earlier to help you prepare for your aligned Third-Level presentation:

> *You said your first objective was to. . . .* Pick one client objective at a time: outcome, risk, speed, effort or disruption, and so on.
>
> *We can help you achieve that better. . . .* Name and give a brief description of your branded approach.
>
> *It is different because. . . .* Explain what you do differently from the competition (difference).
>
> *That's important because. . . .* Describe how your difference better achieves the execution objective (preference).
>
> *For example. . . .* 1. Present a relevant story about a client who was in a similar situation; 2. Offer a benchmark that shows that your difference led to a measurably better outcome; and 3. Offer a specific client comment that speaks to how your difference helped them achieve this objective (proof).
>
> *Before I move to your next objective I would like to make sure we have addressed your first objective. Have we addressed this to your satisfaction?* (verification and agreement)
>
> *You said another important objective was to. . . .* repeat as above.

The following is the example from a broker positioning statement we showed you earlier where the client's principle execution objective was speed.

> *You said that your first objective was* to complete this transaction as soon as possible to release funds for another opportunity.

We can get you the fastest execution because we will use our Private Investor execution.

It's different because where most brokers slowly roll out the property to a narrow market in order to protect their commission, we will immediately show this property not only to our database of buyers, but also to all brokers, including those from other firms, and share commissions.

That is important to you because it attracts the most buyers quickly. It puts pressure on the buyers to move faster because they know another buyer is standing in the wings.

For example, we recently inherited a property from another brokerage firm that had been on the market for six months. Using our Private Investor execution, we found a buyer in three weeks. That buyer was from another city and was brought in by another firm. The seller told us that our fast execution "saved my job. I only wish I new about you sooner."

Before I move to your next objective I would like to make sure we have addressed your concerns about completing this as quickly as possible. Have we addressed this to your satisfaction?

You said another objective was to get the highest price for this asset.

Again, the purpose of scripting is to provide a discipline to your presentation to assure you are addressing objective, difference, preference, and proof. Use the scripting to build your presentation, then use your own more natural wording to present it.

Who Should Present?

All too frequently the presentation is dominated by the senior person and not the professionals who will execute it. Generally speaking, those doing the work should do the presenting because they are the ones who need to make an emotional connection with the client. Remember your clients are buying a relationship.

A service buyer, who was conducting RFP interviews, told me about a presentation that should have been left to the executing broker. The broker brought one of the senior members of his firm along. The client welcomed the support of the broker's senior management, but in this case the senior executive dominated the conversation but knew little about the specifics of the project. He dropped names and told anecdotal stories for the entire session. The well-qualified broker never got a chance to make his case and so he did not win the business.

To review, clients want to work with partners who understand them best. You create maximum preference by aligning your unique service capabilities to the prospective client's unique perception of value. Share what you learned that is unique about the client first.

DELIBERATE PRACTICE: THIRD-LEVEL PROPOSALS AND PRESENTATIONS

A vendor-centric proposal asks clients to learn more about you. A client-centric proposal shares what you have learned about the client and then aligns your capabilities to fit this client's differentiators. Now we can combine the work you did to accelerate your message with the work you did to differentiate on the client to build an aligned client-centric proposal and presentation. To build your client-centric proposal or recommendation, harvest the client differentiation content from your client profile. Use the following format to build your presentation.

(Client Differentiation)

Project/Property/Preference Difference

1. Client execution concerns, causes, and impact
2. Client objectives, timeframes, and constraints
3. Verification: "Is that correct? What has changed?"

(Aligned Vendor Differentiation)

Your Aligned Difference

1. Your unique approach/solution (Branded where possible)
2. Difference (What is different about your approach?)
3. Preference (Why difference is important to this client's objectives)
4. Proof (Story, benchmark, specific testimonial that this client will achieve his/her objective)

Chapter 10

Pricing and Third-Level Negotiation

Decision Hierarchy

Client Differentiators: 3rd Level

1. *Personal Relationship*
2. *Professional Relationship*
3. *Property/Project Difference*
4. *Preference Difference*
5. *Process Difference*

Vendor Differentiators: 2nd Level

6. *Proof*
7. *Experience*
8. *Approach*
9. *Capabilities*

10. Price

Figure 10.1 Sometimes the Decision Hierarchy Feels More Like This.

Although it is the last differentiator, price is going to come up sooner or later, and when it does, it will feel like the only differentiator. It's like the elephant in the room. Even when commission rates are fixed, somehow price becomes a sticking point. For clients who are frequently in the market it could be the first

131

question they ask: "What would your rate be for this?" Serious price negotiation usually occurs late in the decision process.

WE LOST ON PRICE?

I like to ask my workshop audiences how many of them lost business recently because of price. Most hands go up. Then I ask how many of them won their last deal because of price. Almost no hands go up. Isn't it interesting that we perceive we lose because of price, but when we win, it is because of something we did to change the outcome?

In any service provider decision the majority of competitors lose. The reason most often cited, "We lost on price." Claiming to have lost on price saves face for a rejected service provider. For clients buying a service, telling the losing bidder that price was the deciding factor is also the easy way out. Clients don't risk offending anyone by saying that they didn't think a service provider could do the job as well, and they avoid getting into arguments with vendors about the real reason they chose the winning firm.

If price were the real reason for losing, that would mean that the winner won on price. But how often have you heard someone say they won because of price? When price is the deciding factor, it is because the service buyer worked through the buying hierarchy—the client and vendor differentiators—and perceived no difference between the finalists. That means you are by definition a commodity. Is that possible? I don't think so.

In my opinion if a human is highly involved in delivering a service, the service can't be a commodity. Think about the role of a waiter for example. You bring water, take drink orders, take food orders, deliver food, take plates away, and collect on the bill. If any service job is a commodity that would be it, particularly when compared to the complex role of a real estate service provider.

But all of us have had the unfortunate experience of having a very expensive dinner ruined by poor service, or having a simple dinner significantly improved by a top-notch waitperson. In fact the latter is more likely to happen since our expectations are much higher for an expensive dinner.

The point is that if the relatively simple and common role of a waiter can have such dramatically different outcomes, think about the differences for your more complex service delivery. Anything that involves humans cannot be a commodity, so commoditization must be self-inflicted.

If you say you lost on price, you are really saying you were unable to differentiate your service to justify your price premium. In fact, in most cases, the reason for losing out to competitors is not price; instead, it is the failure to establish preference in the mind of the service buyer.

Remember that price difference, like value, is in the eyes of the beholder. Some clients view a 10 percent price variation as comparable. Others view even one basis point as a premium.

"WHO WOULD YOU CHOOSE IF PRICES WERE THE SAME?"

Here is a way to isolate price in your negotiations and force your competitors to compete on price. If the client suggests that you sharpen your pencil to match a competitor's price, ask the client who they would choose if prices were the same. You are in effect commoditizing price as a decision factor and forcing the client back up the hierarchy.

If you are the chosen provider when price is commoditized, ask the client why. They will probably offer a differentiator (relationship, understanding, rank, approach) up the hierarchy: "I like you better," "you understand my business or this asset better," and so on.

Next ask the client how important that difference is. What would it mean to them if these advantages where not available?

Now ask the client what that difference is worth. Maybe you can negotiate a few basis points more.

If you are getting the last look, or if you are chosen at the same price, then you are forcing your competitor to compete on price. In order to win, your competition always has to find a price below yours to buy back that client's preference. If you are getting last looks, you are not competing on price. They are.

THIRD-LEVEL NEGOTIATING

"I may not be a good poker player, but if you show me your hand before I have to bet, I am going to win a lot more."

Rich Hake is the founder of Kipling Capital, a private capital real estate investment firm. Referring to negotiating and knowing your client better, Rich once said to me, "I may not be a good poker player, but if you show me your hand before I have to bet, I am going to win a lot more."

I don't hold myself to be an expert on negotiations, but I do know that the more you know your client (client differentiation) the more leverage you will have. Let's take a look at each of the five client differentiators to see how they can help you better negotiate the terms of your services.

Personal Relationship

Your personal relationship with the client is your best protection against price pressure. Think again about your own experience hiring service professionals. How much harder is it to play hardball with a friend than a vendor? At the very least a friend will tell you where you need to be on price so that you don't leave money on the table. In most cases though, your client friend won't push too hard on your pricing as long as it is reasonable and justifiable.

Be careful not to take advantage of your friends though. If your client friend finds out they are paying considerably more than the market, your friendship may be threatened, and you will be forced to compete on the next deal.

The other side of the risk is that your client may take advantage of your friendship to get better pricing from you. I suggest you tell your friendly client that, if it were up to you, they would get below-cost pricing, but that you are already giving them the best pricing that senior management will allow. Make someone else the heavy.

Professional Relationship

Tim Meissner is a founding principal in Meissner Jacquet Investment Management Services, San Diego's second largest commercial property management company. The company has a prestigious roster of clients including some top institutional players. Tim's challenge is to get full value for services that some of the national organizations provide at cost to win other service fees.

When I interviewed Tim for the book, he was in the middle of a negotiation with a potential client who clearly preferred Meissner Jacquet but was having trouble with the 25 percent premium price. Another competitor was offering their services at what Tim considered unacceptably low margins. Tim knew that to win the business he would have to focus the client's attention on value difference instead of price difference.

As part of his sales effort, Tim acquired a deep understanding of this client's strategic objectives. He knew that the client wanted to outsource asset management so that the principals of the client firm could focus on growing their portfolio. The property management side was too time consuming and was slowing their growth.

To get them to think more about value than price, Tim asked the client why he preferred Meissner Jacquet. The client answered that he felt that Tim's company was more likely to handle the job with the least oversight. That would allow the principals to completely offload the work. Then Tim asked the client what it would mean to them to be free of that burden. The client said that the company could better focus on core competencies and grow faster. Tim then asked what would happen if the chosen asset manager wasn't able to handle things without intervention. The client said that it would defeat the whole purpose of outsourcing.

Tim used his knowledge of the client's strategic objectives to position his firm's value. Instead of haggling over a $25 per hour difference in service cost, Tim kept the focus on the value of the client's principal's time. In that context saving $25 per hour seemed trivial.

Strategic issues almost always dwarf price differences. If you can keep the focus on the objectives instead of the price difference, you should be able to negotiate a premium. For example, a lender client, who was in final negotiations on pricing, was told that his fees were higher than his competitor's. The lender reminded his client that the objective was to improve cash flow and that this structure left the client with more cash even though it was a bit more expensive. That ended the price negotiation.

Knowing More About The Project or Property

Lori Johanson of Citi Realty Services told me about choosing a broker for one challenging lease renewal negotiation. Several of the competing brokers recommended an immediate and aggressive renegotiation before market conditions changed. But they didn't say how they would create leverage. They didn't know the unique circumstances of this building and this owner. Lori felt these brokers where operating with an ax and she needed someone with a scalpel because the situation was more nuanced than that.

Citi chose the broker who knew more about the building owner (the lessor) and Citi's (the lessee) unique situation. The winning broker knew that the building owners were looking to sell the property, and would have to achieve the renewal lease rates in their pro-forma cash flows to investors. He also knew that Citi used GAAP accounting so that total cost including tenant improvements was more important than the simple lease rate.

Citi was willing to accept a higher rental rate, which was more important to the landlord, as long as tenant improvements and other concessions would get them to the right overall cost. That knowledge gave the winning broker room to negotiate better overall terms that fit the bank and the owner.

Knowing More About Decision Maker Preferences

Chris Ludeman is now president of America's Brokerage for CB Richard Ellis, but when he was a young broker negotiating to purchase a large piece of property, he used his deep knowledge of the seller's financial needs and preferences to gain leverage in a challenging negotiation. Chris was assembling a large piece of property for a buyer who needed to get the transaction completed quickly. The seller of one of the key pieces was moving slowly, and a key decision maker was off playing golf at Pebble Beach. Chris' client sent him up to Pebble on a private plane.

The seller lit into Chris for interrupting his vacation. Chris said he let the seller rant on for a number of minutes, then pulled out the contracts and said, "I am leaving in five minutes with or without your signature. But if you don't sign it, you won't be able to put the $25 million gain in this quarter's financials." The seller smiled and signed the papers.

Chris had known the purchase price paid by this owner and also knew the CFO of the selling company wanted this gain to offset some weaknesses in their financials in the current quarter. That deep knowledge of the property and the seller's preferences gave Chris the confidence and leverage to win.

Knowing More About The Decision Process

I am frequently asked by workshop participants how to avoid lower-level decision makers. Real estate service providers often find themselves forced to work with someone below the real decision makers, and it is hard to go around lower-level staff without risking making them angry.

As decision makers see less risk in their decision, they tend to delegate those decisions to others or make their decision based upon price. Further, these lower-level decision makers view their role as mostly negotiators since shortlisted vendors offer similar capabilities. In their minds success means getting the lowest price or best terms.

If decision makers don't feel the pain, your ability to differentiate on anything other than price is limited. Therefore the risk of alienating the lower-level influencer is almost always outweighed by the importance of getting to real decision makers. The bottom line is that you have to get to the decision maker and differentiate on them in order to build preference up the decision hierarchy. And it starts with the RFP process.

The request for proposal process is usually driven by a lower-level influencer. Responding firms are frequently not allowed to meet with real decision makers until the short list presentations.

This system creates a distinct advantage for the market leader because market leaders, particularly dominant players, often get a free pass to the short list.

If you are not the market leader, I would strongly recommend that you not respond to the RFP without a face-to-face meeting. In order to do that you will have to prepare and present a strong argument as to why it is in the client's interests to meet with you early in the process.

One company that I worked with used the following argument: "Each of our clients is unique and so are our recommended solutions. We would never offer you a generic solution to your situation. Therefore, we can only respond to requests for proposals where we have a rich understanding of your situation and objectives."

If and when you get the face-to-face meeting, remember, even if they view your services as the same, as we have demonstrated often in this book, there is still plenty of room to differentiate on the client.

In summary, if you were truly a commodity, you would have no pricing power. In order to win the business, you would have to be the lowest-price player. When the client has no execution concerns or personal or professional attachment to any of the alternative service providers, it's challenging if not impossible to establish preference. Price will drive the decision.

But you are not a commodity because the services that you perform are complex and highly variable. So don't accept the commodity label even in a highly competitive environment.

Most clients are willing to pay a little more if they perceive that you are different and better, particularly if you rank the highest. But they are also willing to pay more if they know, like, and trust you and if you understand them better. Your knowledge of their unique situation also gives you leverage.

Once you have differentiated on the client, you can now commoditize price by asking who they would choose if prices were the same. Force the client back up the hierarchy. This causes clients to think about value difference instead of focusing on price difference.

DELIBERATE PRACTICE: PRICING AND THIRD-LEVEL NEGOTIATION

You gain leverage in negotiations by knowing more about your client. Acquiring clients at the Third Level is not only the best way to win their business, but it is also the best way to win favorable terms. All of your deliberate practice will help you gain leverage in negotiations, but here are a few specifics to work on:

- Commoditize price: Ask clients who they would choose if prices and terms were the same. If they don't say that they would choose you under those circumstances, you are in trouble. Your only advantage now is price. If they do say that they would choose you, ask them why. Then ask them what that difference is worth or how close to the cover bid you need to come in.

- Get to decision makers: Prepare and practice your best argument about why it is in the best interest of your client that you meet face-to-face before you submit a proposal. If the client still resists, move on to your next opportunity, preferably one where you are the one who sets the RFP specs. We will show you how to do that in the next chapter about winning in the invisible market.

PART III

Winning without Competition

In Part I, I showed you that winning goes well beyond selling. Once the client has decided to use the services that you and others provide, their only remaining decision is which service provider to choose. I showed you how to accelerate your message to create and position your value proposition against competitors. In Part II I showed you how elite providers win in competition by differentiating on and aligning to client differentiators. In Part III I will show you how to avoid competition altogether first by delighting clients so that they would never consider working with anyone but you and then by acquiring new clients in the "invisible market" before the project gets competitive.

Chapter 11

Third-Level Client Satisfaction

By far the best way to win in competition is to delight the clients that you already have. Relationship not only drives the choice of service provider in new client acquisitions, it is also the biggest driver of client satisfaction and retention. In fact, the drivers of client satisfaction and retention are the same Third-Level principles employed to win the business in the first place.

HIGHLY SATISFIED (VERSUS SATISFIED) CLIENTS TWICE AS LOYAL

Keeping clients is frequently more important than winning new ones. Even a fast-growing concern realizes 80 percent of its revenues from existing clients. However client loyalty has never been more difficult to attain. Traditional service satisfaction attributes like experience, capability, timeliness, thoroughness, responsiveness, and so on have become minimum requirements and are no longer differentiators. They are table stakes in a more competitive world.

Today if you want clients who are loyal advocates, they must be highly satisfied. Highly satisfied clients arise from a deeper personal and strategic partnership. If your goal is just a satisfied client, you are setting your sights far too low. Satisfied clients invite you to compete again. But highly satisfied clients not only give you follow-on business (frequently sole sourced); they also actively refer you to others. They become in effect a surrogate sales force.

Highly satisfied clients are also far more profitable. According to Fred Reichheld, director emeritus of Bain & Company and author of *Loyalty Rules* and *The Ultimate Question*, a 5 percent increase in client retention can lead to a 25–95 percent increase in company profits!

What's the difference between highly satisfied and just satisfied clients?

We recently conducted a study for ValleyCrest, a major player in the commercial landscape development and maintenance sector, to determine the difference between a *highly satisfied* client and a *satisfied* client because their own research showed that highly satisfied clients were more than twice as likely to be repeat customers.

We discovered that both satisfied and highly satisfied clients used similar language to describe qualifications and execution

Loyalty Effect

- A **5 percent** increase in customer retention can lead to a **25-95 percent increase** in company profits.
  Fred Reichheld, *Loyalty Rules*

- **Who is loyal? Why?**
  - **81 percent** of the **highly satisfied**
  - **35 percent** of the **satisfied** group and
  - **2 percent** of the **less than satisfied**

Figure 11.1 Highly Satisfied Clients Are More Profitable and More Loyal.

effectiveness. Comments like capable, responsive, thorough, and on time and on budget were common with both groups.

Highly satisfied customers however were much more likely to name a specific professional and use emotional language like comfort, trust, partner, team member, and so on. They also were more likely to comment on value added contributions related to a deeper knowledge on the part of the service provider of the unique aspects of the project, client situation, and preferences.

Interestingly, highly satisfied clients were just as likely as satisfied clients to complain about some aspect of the project execution indicating that highly satisfied clients were also more likely

SATISFIED CLIENT COMMENTS	HIGHLY SATISFIED COMMENTS
QUALIFICATIONS COMMENTS:	**RELATIONSHIP COMMENTS:**
Professional	Named specific service provider
Qualified	Long working relationship
Knowledgeable	Good people
Industry leader	Supporting partner
Experienced	Working team member
	Delight to work with
	Trust, forthright, and honest
EXECUTION COMMENTS:	**VALUE ADDED COMMENTS:**
Responsive	Understand what we are looking for
Excellent work	Made my job easier
Good follow through	Proactive
Did what they said	Good listener
Smooth process	Better ideas and solutions
Efficient	Helped with design
Met requirements	Good at troubleshooting
Competitive, fair price	Creative
Within budget	

Figure 11.2 Take Care of It to Satisfy. Take Care of Them to Highly Satisfy.

to forgive. That makes sense when you consider that it is easier to fire a vendor than a friend. It also explains why competitors have a harder time breaking into a strategic relationship with a highly satisfied client.

TAKE CARE OF IT (SATISFIED) AND TAKE CARE OF ME (HIGHLY SATISFIED)

In Chapter 2 we used the Decision Funnel to describe how clients choose a service provider. (See Figure 11.3)

You will recall that clients first ask, "Who can do it?" to create a set of alternatives. When the search phase yields choice it allows clients to ask, "Who can take care of it better?" to screen out

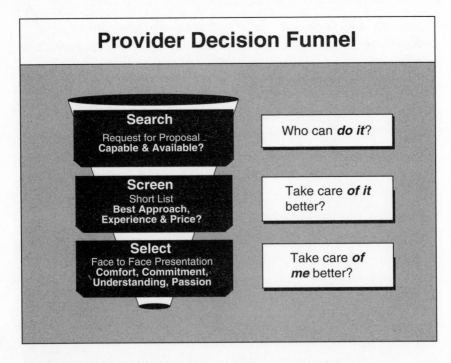

Figure 11.3 "Take Care of Me," to Win the Business and to Achieve Higher Satisfaction.

weaker options. To pick the first among equals during the selection phase, clients ask, "Who will take care of me better?" It turns out that the attributes that caused clients to choose you in the first place are the same ones that drive client satisfaction.

At the end of the day clients only have two satisfaction criteria: 1) Did you take care of it? and 2) Did you take care of me? If you did the former, you created a satisfied client. You will be included in their short list of qualified vendors for future business. If you did both, you created a highly satisfied client, who will likely award you follow-on business with little or no competition.

"Taking care of it" speaks to your capability and execution effectiveness (Level 2). You met the specs, your price was competitive, you were responsive and completed the work on time and on budget. Clients are satisfied when you do that. (Dissatisfied clients are angry that you did not meet these minimum expectations. Dissatisfied clients are five times less likely to repeat when compared to even satisfied clients.)

On the other hand "taking care of me" means you have established a personal and strategic relationship with the client and an understanding of their unique project, situation, and preferences better than anyone else (Third Level). That creates confidence and trust that you will assume their burden and protect their position better. Those emotional differentiators are far more important to the client than minor differences in capabilities and experience.

Sometimes the professionals who execute the business are different than the ones who sell it. In lending it's the credit, servicing, and legal departments who get involved after the sale. Professionals who manage the property frequently are not responsible for selling. Builder project mangers, estimators, and superintendents may present at proposal presentations, but they are not usually the primary sales leads. Lead brokers frequently have teams involved in the execution of the sale or lease.

These non-selling professionals are usually surprised to learn that they are more responsible for the company's revenues than the primary sellers. That is because they may have more influence on client satisfaction. If 80 percent or more of the revenues come from existing clients, and if the execution professionals drive client perception of being cared for, then non-selling professionals drive more sales than sales professionals.

So even if you have acquired clients using your sharpened Third-Level skills, your execution team could lose them if they don't use those same skills to delight your clients. So you may want to pass this book on to the non-selling professionals on your team.

Measure Satisfaction to Fix It

There is an old saying in engineering, "You can't fix it if you can't measure it." Most real estate providers do little or no client satisfaction tracking. These companies assume that if they do their job well, (take care of it), that is enough.

Some companies do track client satisfaction, but they only do it after the project is completed when it's too late to fix the relationship. A client who is dissatisfied not only won't give you their business in the future, they also won't recommend you to others. In fact they are probably saying bad things about you in the market.

Companies that closely track and measure client satisfaction not only can fix relationships before they break, they also have better proof statements they can use to win future business.

Earlier we discussed the importance of proof in order to create differentiation and certainty in your message. We said that a good proof statement should include a story about a client in a similar situation, a benchmark showing a better outcome, and a specific testimonial that speaks to how your difference achieved the better outcome. Client satisfaction metrics and comments are another fertile source for proof statements. Delighted clients give great testimony.

DPR Construction is one of the country's largest commercial contractors. DPR not only tracks client satisfaction, they do it three times during the course of a project. They administer their Customer Satisfaction Survey (CSS) during preconstruction, mid-construction, and at close out. By surveying clients early, DPR feels that they fix problems before they get difficult and threaten their hard-earned relationship with the client.

As we have seen, delighting clients not only increases customer loyalty, it makes it easier to win new business. That is because satisfied clients provide the stories, benchmarks, and testimonials that offer proof of your superior capabilities to new clients.

For example, DPR uses its client satisfaction metrics as proof for their positioning statements when competing for new clients. Everybody says they deliver on time and on budget with zero defects and a smooth process that is flexible, client driven, and cost effective. However, few can prove it. Where most commercial contractors are pitching generic capabilities, DPR can prove that they are best in class.

DPR calls it their "virtuous cycle." They use their client satisfaction metrics first to measure and improve execution (see Figure 11.4). As they track improved performance, those metrics provide the evidence that makes it easier for new clients to choose them. In other words DPR's efforts to improve provide the metric byproducts to prove it is better.

REFERRAL: THE BEST MEASURE

Tracking client satisfaction can be as simple as asking one question. In his best selling book, *The Ultimate Question Driving Good*

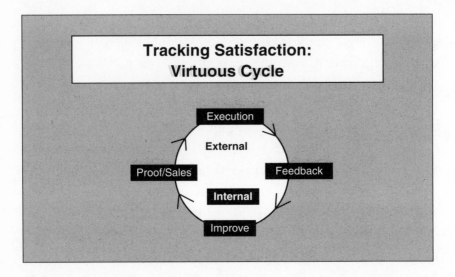

Figure 11.4 Measure to Improve and Prove You Are Better.

Profits and True Growth, author Fred Reichheld suggests that the best indicator of client satisfaction is whether a client would recommend you to someone else. So he suggests that you measure satisfaction by asking clients the ultimate question: "How likely are you to recommend this company to a friend or colleague?"

By asking the ultimate question, you are not only tracking satisfaction, you are also avoiding another cold call. Remember, the best way to avoid a cold call is to get a referral. Once again, that is why elite service providers are not making cold calls. Their delighted clients are selling for them with sole-sourced follow-on business and referrals.

CLIENT ADVOCATES: TAKING CARE OF YOU

Dissatisfied clients threaten your survival. You will not even be allowed to compete for their future business. That revenue will have to be replaced from scratch.

You can survive with satisfied clients, but only with great effort. You will at least be allowed to compete for their future business and include them in your list of clients, but you will have to resell each project and probably compete more on price.

But if you create highly satisfied clients, you will spend much less time selling than your competitors because your delighted clients will assume that burden for you. Not only will they give you their follow-up work, they will sell you to others in the form of recommendations and referrals. You will sell less, win more, and enjoy it more.

Winning the relationship is different from winning the deal. Winning the relationship means successfully completing the project and, by doing so, creating the best possible source of future business—a delighted client. To win the relationship, you are encouraged to expand your Third-Level efforts to establish a team-centric relationship with all of the client stakeholders, especially the client's execution staff.

DELIBERATE PRACTICE: DELIGHTING CLIENTS

- Use all five client differentiators that you used to win the business to build client satisfaction and loyalty. By accelerating personal and professional relationships, clients will feel that you are taking care of them personally. By understanding their project and preferences better, you can add value and unburden the client.
- Track client satisfaction. Whether formally or informally, find a way to measure your client's attitude about your services. Don't stop at the usual indicators that only measure whether you took care of it—just did what was expected.

(*Continued*)

See if you can determine if the client feels that you took care of them.

- The best way to do that is to ask if they would recommend you to someone else. That way you can both track satisfaction and get a referral.

- When tracking client satisfaction, see if you can harvest client metrics and testimonials to use as proof statements for future business development efforts.

Chapter 12

Winning in the Invisible Market

Figure 12.1 Visible and Invisible Market.

My first book, *Winning In The Invisible Market*, focused on avoiding competition by creating the business instead of waiting for it. The idea was to engage clients earlier in their decision process and win the business before it could become competitive. The best way to win in competition is to avoid competition. The best way to avoid competition is to win before the deal ever sees the light of day.

Before they hire you, potential clients make two decisions. They decide they need the services that you and your competitors offer (the service decision), and then they choose you among alternative service providers (the service provider decision).

By the time a company decides to seek outside services and moves into the visible market, it is reaching the end of a multi-phase decision-making process. They have already identified and assessed a problem and envisioned and built internal consensus on a solution. Of primary importance to you is that they often have a preferred service provider in mind—a provider who began supporting them before the project became visible to the rest of the market.

The service decision is made in the invisible market. The service provider decision is made in the visible market. One of the best ways to win the business is to engage clients while they are making the service decisions—build, finance, buy, sell, manage, furnish, and so on—and to establish a preferred provider or sole provider status before the business sees the light of day.

The visible market—the portion of the market comprised of clients actively and openly looking for a real estate service

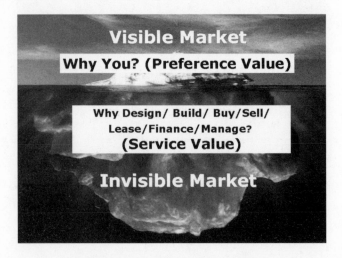

Figure 12.2 Why You?: Visible
Why Your Service?: Invisible.

provider—represents only the tip of the opportunity iceberg (see Figures 12.1 and 12.2).

By the time clients enter your field of vision by taking proactive steps to hire an outside professional—asking for proposals, statements of qualifications, or price quotes—your competition has probably already been there. Yes, the prospects are qualified; you can be assured they are actively seeking the type of services you provide. But unfortunately, in most cases, the prospect already has a preferred provider who usually wins the business. If you are not the preferred provider, the deck is stacked against you.

INVISIBLE MARKET DANGER: UNQUALIFIED CLIENTS

Although the invisible market includes clients in an earlier stage of a service decision, it also includes clients who won't be making either a service or a service provider decision. In fact, in most markets, the majority of suspected clients will not be making a service provider decision any time soon. So there is a high likelihood that you could be wasting your time. Think about the number of cold calls you have made to prospects who didn't need you at that time.

So there is the trade off; the invisible market is where you build sole or preferred provider status, but unlike the visible market where clients have already decided to move forward, most suspects are unqualified. If you are going to be successful in the invisible market you will need to:

1. Gain access to invisible market clients earlier when they are still suspects;
2. Quickly determine if they have the service problems you solve and where they are in the decision process; and

3. Make momentum recommendations that are aligned to their decision stage, advance the decision, and gain commitment from the client to move forward.

Why Your Services?

Your value in the invisible market is different than your value in the visible competitive market. Your value in the visible market is in the problems you solve better than your competitors. Can you do this faster, better, cheaper, with less risk, effort, and disruption than they can?

In the invisible market the client has not yet decided to use your services. So it does not yet matter if you can do it better because they haven't decided to do *it* yet. So here your value proposition is not in the problems you solve better. It is in the problems that you and your competitors solve. In other words clients aren't asking, "Why should I choose you?" In the invisible market they are asking, "Why should I use your services?" The answer is because it solves a service problem or achieves an objective.

No Problem = No Value

In the invisible market your value zone includes the clients who have the problem that your services address. For example, if you are a commercial real estate lender, you may be looking for clients who cannot finance growth through operations because of an inefficient use of capital. A variable rate or asset-backed financing could release cash to pay for growth or investment. If you are a leasing broker, you are looking for clients whose space no longer fits changing business conditions. A new lease or sublease may provide better space fit utilization.

Once you determine what your service value is, then you will want to target and access those potential clients to see if they have the problems you solve.

Gain Access

When you ask a client for a meeting, the client has four questions that must be answered compellingly and succinctly before they will share their time.

1. Who are you?
2. Why do I need you?
3. How are you different?
4. What is the value of this meeting?

1. Who Are You?

That one is easy—it's your pitch. This answer will usually include your name, company, position, and role. Obviously if the client already knows and likes you, getting a meeting is not that challenging. Also, if you know someone in common who referred you, your chances of getting the meeting are significantly increased. Finally if you have done work for someone else in the industry or market, that will add to your credibility and their curiosity.

2. Why Do I Need You?

This one is a bit trickier. Remember, your value is in the problems that you solve, not in your capability. Yet most providers define themselves by their capabilities: "I help my clients buy, sell, lease, manage, finance, and design property." Instead, focus on the problems you solve and the objectives clients have. For example, instead of just saying you are a leasing broker, add that you work with clients whose space no longer fits changing business conditions.

When I am talking to a potential client, I don't just say that I am a sales trainer or a sales strategy consultant. I tell them that I work with clients who face increasing competition and want to improve their win rate and avoid competing on price. I focus on the problem that makes my capability valuable.

3. How Are You Different?

In many if not most cases the client already has or knows a service provider so they will want to know how you are different to determine if this is a good use of their time. What will this client get from you that they may not get from other providers? What do you do differently, or better yet, what problems do you solve differently? Here you can use some of your preference value differentiators, particularly your proof statements that we worked on in Chapter 3.

4. What Is the Value of This Meeting?

A meeting is a transaction. Unless both parties perceive that they are getting value, the meeting will not happen. Yet most requests for meetings are one-sided transactions. "I would like to understand your situation and get to know your company." The client is hearing, "I want to take your time to have you tell me something about your company so that I can sell you something you don't need now." The client wants to know what they are going to get out of it. The client knows what you want. What are you offering for their time?

Always try to give something before you ask for something. You are in the market as much or more than your clients. Although they know what is going on with their asset, they don't have your view of the broader market. Why not share that broader view. Not just research. Take a position or a point of view.

For example, a managing director of a brokerage firm told me a story of how two new brokers used this point-of-view technique to quickly access and build their reputation in their market. Initially they took company research, created a three-page white paper on the market, and then asked potential clients if they could come in and share their POV of property trends in the client's market. With each meeting their expertise, reputation, and relationships grew creating another virtuous cycle. These new brokers quickly became the biggest hitters in the office, a feat that normally would have taken years.

One real estate client I interviewed told me that he would meet with anyone who could tell him something about his market, his competition, or his company that he did not know. Use your knowledge as a quid pro quo for a meeting and watch your cold-calling efforts improve dramatically.

Jim Tucker, a very successful retail broker for Sperry Van Ness in Richmond, Virginia, is a strong believer in giving something away before asking for something. Jim offers retail property owners a full competitive analysis. The owners are frequently shocked by the level of detail in Jim's analysis, and they are all but certain to include Jim on their short list of brokers when the time comes to buy or sell.

DOES THIS CLIENT HAVE THE PROBLEMS YOU SOLVE?

Once you have gained access and accelerated your personal and professional relationship, your primary objective is to determine if this suspect has the problems that you solve. Remember though that problems and therefore your service value is in the eyes of the beholder. If they don't think they have a problem, then your services hold no value.

You will recall the strategic questioning strategy that used a give-and-take change question to uncover strategic problems that we covered earlier. Once the client revealed a strategic problem, we suggested probing the problem deeper by looking for CID— cause, impact, done, doing, considering.

To determine if this client has the problems that you solve use the problem/CID questioning strategy, but this time load the question with a give-and-take question that speaks to the problem that your service addresses. This service value questioning strategy is shown in Figure 12.3.

The difference is that you will want to frame give-and-take questions that speak to the service problems that you can support, and if the client has those problems, then explore them for CID.

Service Partnering
(Invisible Market Questioning Strategy)

1. Problem Questions (Service Value)
   (Give and Take — Service Problem?)

2. Probe Problems for CID:
   • Cause? (Can you help?)
   • Impact? (Criticality & Urgency?)
   • Done/Doing/Considering? (Resistance?)

3. Gaining Agreement to Explore Solutions
   • Feedback & Convert to and Verify Objective
   • "Would you be interested in exploring…"

Figure 12.3 Use Partnering Questions to Qualify Invisible Market Suspects.

For example a lender might frame the following give-and-take question to uncover a problem that financing could support: "Many of my clients are facing narrowing margins that are making it harder to finance operations and growth, what changes are you seeing?"

If this client shares a problem related to financing, the lender would follow up with CID questions. Once again, good company research is the best way to frame give-and-take questions. The leasing broker who has done her homework might ask, "John, I read in the *Business Times* that you moving some of your operations to lower costs. How are your space requirements changing?"

If the problems that you uncover are ones that you can support, then convert them to objectives and get permission to explore solutions.

"John, you said that you were moving operations in order to lower costs and increase margins. But that change would leave you with a surplus of space here, and that would keep your costs high. So your objective is to reduce your cost of real estate by reducing the burden of unused space. Is that right?

Would you be interested in exploring ways to lower your real estate costs?"

Before you make a recommendation find out more about the existing property, this client's preferences, and decision process. You will also want to determine where they are in their decision process and how motivated they are to fix the problem. Remember, you are a partner now, not a vendor.

FINDING AND ALIGNING TO THE SERVICE DECISION

In the invisible market you are engaging clients earlier in their decision process, so you will need to understand and be able to read where clients are in order to make appropriate recommendations to move forward. You probably will not get a signed contract in your first meeting. In the following section, I will show you why and how clients make service decisions and how you can align to those decisions and influence them in your favor.

Clients, like the rest of us, have hundreds of problems. Only critical and urgent problems lead to action. To qualify your opportunities you need to be able to read where your client is in their decision process and determine when and if they are going to act.

The Five Stages of the Service Decision

Decisions tend to follow a pattern. If you can recognize that pattern and locate your prospect in the process, it will be easier to make appropriate recommendations that advance the decision (see Figure 12.4). The following are the stages to a prospect's service decision.

Problems become objectives in a predictable manner and tend to go through five stages once a problem has been identified:

- *Stage 1: Problem Awareness* – The company begins to perceive a threat or opportunity.
- *Stage 2: Problem Assessment* – Analysis of the threat is initiated. You can tell that a problem has advanced to this point when there is a metric attached to it. "Our real estate costs have risen 20 percent." Another indicator of this stage is that

5 DECISION STAGES

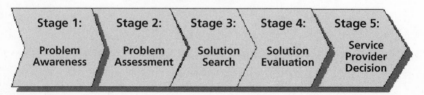

Figure 12.4 Decisions to Use Your Services Go Through 5 Stages.

the problem becomes an objective. If the threat is considered significant enough, it becomes a priority and objectives are set.

- *Stage 3: Solution Search* – A search for a solution is undertaken and the client attempts to expand his universe of alternatives.
- *Stage 4: Evaluation Solution* – Alternatives are narrowed and evaluated for best fit and a course of action is chosen.
- *Stage 5: Service Provider Decision* – Clients search for, screen, and then select a service provider to execute the project.

If you are pursuing clients in the invisible market, you have to be careful not to waste your time with suspects who can't or won't make a decision. Clients in the early stages of a service decision are not yet ready to sign up for your services. They need to work their way through the decision process with smaller steps before they are ready to choose you and your services.

Your ability to quickly read and then escort their decision process is critical to winning in the invisible market. Therefore most of your recommendations in the invisible market will be momentum recommendations—incremental recommendations to move to the next stage of the decision.

Momentum Recommendations

Has this ever happened to you? The prospect seemed interested in your solution, so you tell the prospect you will put something in writing and get back to her. You send in your proposal and wait for a response. Nothing. You call. No response. You wait an appropriate period. You reach her voice mail. "Ellen, I just wanted to follow up on that proposal . . . ." No response.

When this happens to you, it's because the excitement of finding a problem that you could solve distracted you from converting value into action through a momentum recommendation. As soon as you left the prospect's office, your biggest and most dangerous competitor—the status quo—won back your prospect's attention and affection.

A potential client's motivation to act peaks during face-to-face meetings. Your presence shines a light on a problem and a possible resolution. If you do not convert that motivation into action, you may have lost your best opportunity to win the business. At the very least, by failing to keep momentum and gain commitment, you have extended the decision and potentially opened the door for your competitors.

The decisions you want your client to make are typically complex and can take months or even years to culminate in the choice of a service provider. By keeping the engagement process moving forward, you increase the likelihood of success and reduce your cost of sales.

Building momentum and commitment over an extended decision process requires making momentum recommendations that:

1. Are in alignment with the prospect's current stage in the service decision process (see previous decision stages);
2. Advance the decision; and
3. Require the prospect to act now.

Momentum recommendations continually advance the engagement, build motivation, clarify and build preference for your solutions, and build commitment by having the potential client take immediate action. Progress should be measured by where the prospect is in the decision process and what the client must do to move forward.

It's up to you to determine what a realistic recommendation is for the prospect at any given point in the process. In other words, given the client's current decision stage, what can you realistically recommend that will build commitment and momentum? For example, if the prospect is aware of the problem, but has not assessed the risk, what would you recommend they do?

Setting Meeting Recommendation Objectives Before the Call

Whenever you meet with a prospect, establish in advance what the potential minimum and maximum momentum recommendations might be and practice them. Make sure you have a recommendation in mind even if it is only to set another meeting. What is the outcome of the recommendation, and why would that be of value to your prospect?

How will you explain the steps of your recommendation to build clarity and comfort that the outcome will be achieved? Again, urgency is your strongest ally. Look for impending events and gain agreement on a deadline or at least a timeline. Plan your

Momentum Recommendations

(Best outcome? Least outcome?)

Recommendation that is:

1. Aligned with Decision Stage
2. Advances the decision
3. Requires the client to take action

Figure 12.5 Keep the Decision Moving Until the Deal Is Signed.

meeting to assure you have time to present, discuss, and make a plan for implementing that recommendation.

If you engage a client before they are choosing among competitors, you will have a better opportunity to differentiate on the client. When and if competitors get involved, you will already be holding the two most important cards: relationship and client knowledge. That should give you a huge advantage.

The risk of trying to win clients in the invisible market is that you have to kiss a whole bunch of frogs to find a qualified opportunity. And your selling cycle will be longer as the client works through decision stages. Therefore, it is critical that you are able to quickly access and qualify opportunities by reading decision stage and motivation and then making appropriate recommendations that advance the decision and build commitment and preference.

Your reward is a significantly higher win rate, more sole-sourced business, higher fees, and more committed client partners.

DELIBERATE PRACTICE: WINNING IN THE INVISIBLE MARKET

- Problems versus Capabilities. Convert your capabilities message into one that speaks to problems solved and objectives achieved. What are the critical and urgent problems that you and your competitors solve for your clients?

- Write and practice a give-and-take question that you would ask a suspect client to determine if they had the problem you address.

- Practice follow-up questions to uncover CID—cause, impact, done, doing, considering.

- Create a point of view to share with new clients. What do you know about the market that potential clients may not know? Ask your peers where they think the market is headed. Create five to seven PowerPoint slides and then offer to share your POV with your current clients. Ask for their views and include their insights in your expanding POV. Now you are ready to offer your POV to new clients. I think you will find them far more receptive to meeting with you.

- Think about an existing invisible market opportunity. Can you identify what decision stage it is in? What are the indications?

- What momentum recommendation would you make that:

  1. Is aligned with the current decision stage;

  2. Advances the decision to the next stage; and

  3. Gains commitment from the client to take immediate action?

Chapter 13

Managing Third-Level Selling Skills

Most book readers feel that they get a lot out of a book if they find two or three pearls of wisdom that they can apply to their situation. I am trying to shoot higher than that with this book. I am trying to motivate and enable real estate professionals to perform at an elite level. In that respect you and I have the same objective since you achieve success through the success of those that you manage.

As I presented in the first chapter, knowledge is not behavior. Knowing something does not mean that you can do it. Books can create awareness, but that usually does not translate into behavior change unless the reader has been diligent with the suggested deliberate practice. Training workshops and deliberate practice create competence, but unless reinforced regularly in the field, there is a significant risk that skill mastery will not be consistently achieved.

That's where you come in. Behavior change is accomplished by motivated learners with continuous deliberate practice, monitoring, and feedback in the real world. In this chapter I will share some ideas for motivating, monitoring, coaching, and enabling the success of the professionals that you manage.

First I will share ideas to motivate change, since without motivation your people will continue with the behaviors that have locked them into mediocrity. Next I will show you how to use the client profile to track and coach performance. The biggest challenge for any coach is to motivate learning a new skill, so let's start there.

TRACK PERFORMANCE METRICS TO DRIVE THIRD-LEVEL BEST PRACTICES

We have all developed routines at work that we feel make us productive and competent at what we do. Methods and business habits become a well-worn path of business processes that give us a sense of comfort and control over our professional environment. Old work habits are extremely difficult to change, so the motivation to abandon them must be high. People will not change their behavior unless they have solid evidence that their current behavior is not working.

In other words, service providers need a very good reason to improve their current practices. Performance metrics help build that motivation. Poor performers are actually easier to motivate than high-medium performers. Things are going pretty well for them so why change? On the other hand migrating average performers to elite performers offers the highest payoff for your managing efforts.

Service providers who do not believe that their behavior is responsible for poor performance, or that improving it will contribute to better performance, will naturally resist your efforts to make changes. Most professionals believe that a fall off in business is caused by a market slump and is therefore something they can't control.

The market is, in effect, masking poor performance just when the firm needs all hands on deck for superior performance. Once again, if they don't believe their actions can affect the outcome, they will make no effort to improve them.

What's My Motivation?

So how do you build awareness of poor performance and the motivation to change sales practices? Answer: Measure and compare peer performance. Create a scoreboard.

Start with the big activities and refine your scoreboard as you go along. For example, track how many RFPs are received, responded to, and won. Measure the business that comes from new clients versus existing clients. Inventory new business or cross-selling activities, and then share those metrics. Identifying, measuring, and communicating success via metrics builds awareness of both poor and superior performance at every level of selling. The numbers will speak for themselves.

Just make sure that the metrics are relevant to individual performers. As Jack Welch put it in *Straight from the Gut,* "What you measure is what you get ... By *not* aligning measurements and rewards, you often get what you are *not* looking for."

Here's a specific example of how the right metrics can drive performance in your environment. Rank the following statements by how much they would motivate you to make a change in the way you pursue new business.

1. Revenues are not what they should be.
2. Company revenues are off by 30 percent.
3. Your area of personal revenue responsibility is 30 percent below your peers.
4. Next month there will be a firm-wide meeting to discuss peer revenue performance.

The first statement is not a score. It is vague and not personally relevant. You are probably not going to make any major changes, in large part because you're not sure what's causing the problem or what your personal accountability is. The second statement is a measurement, but unless you happen to be the senior executive responsible for firm-wide revenue, it is interesting but not substantially motivating. Your performance may only remotely affect the number, up or down.

However, when you discover that your personal performance is 30 percent below your peers, alarm bells go off and your competitive juices start to flow. Finally, when you discover that your performance will be compared publicly to that of your peers, you have touched off the two most powerful change motivators, competitive spirit and peer prestige.

Most of us are highly driven by competition and prestige. Once we know specifically how we compare, and that we are being compared, most of us will do everything in our power to improve that metric. So, to be effective measurement must be personally relevant. The person who has to change must believe that his or her activities contribute to failure or can affect a positive outcome. Once you have established effective performance measurements, keep refining and sharing the results.

If you are not measuring and tracking performance, you are missing out on one of the most effective ways to change and improve the business development practices of your professionals. Surprisingly, few managers are leveraging the natural motivators of competition and prestige to change business development performance. Operating without metrics is like playing a game without a score. You may have fun, but you won't play as well and you won't improve.

Performance metrics build accountability and release powerful competitive forces that will make your job easier and the outcome more certain for your firm. Once you have instilled motivation for change and identified the behavior (Third-Level Selling skills) that lead to success, the next step is to coach to the results of the behavior.

COACHING RESULTS NOT JUST BEHAVIOR

As the manager, you may think the best way to coach is to make sure that your people are using the questions suggested in this book. That is not necessarily so. You will get better results if you manage to the outcome, not just the behavior.

For example, if one of your sales people is not using the questions that I have recommended, but is consistently finding and building on common ground, then they are getting Third-Level results even if they are not demonstrating the specific behavior. It is the result that is important.

On the other hand, if you find that one or more of the five client differentiators is lacking, now you can coach to the specific questions as a way to get better results. For example, if one of the people you manage is great at accelerating relationships, but consistently misses client preferences, have them practice questions that uncover previous client experiences, current concerns, client visions, and competition with the questions I recommend.

Following is a summary of performance concerns and performance objectives from the book. It will tell you what you are looking for and why you are looking for it.

Third Level™ Teaching Points and Observable Performance Objectives

TEACHING POINT	PERFORMANCE ISSUE	PERFORMANCE OBJECTIVE
DEFINING AND FINDING VALUE	Sales Representative (SR) may lack understanding of value (how and why clients choose them), which adds unnecessary friction throughout their selling efforts.	Understand value (Motivation – Resistance), how clients choose a service, and how they choose among service providers (Decision Funnel).

(Continued)

TEACHING POINT	PERFORMANCE ISSUE	PERFORMANCE OBJECTIVE
PERSONAL RELATIONSHIP ACCELERATION: FINDING COMMON GROUND	Existing relationships increase win rate 200 to 300 percent and lead to higher retention. Yet many SRs do not systematically establish and/or build on common ground.	In client meetings, SR systematically establishes or reestablishes personal common ground. Clients willingly share personal information.
PROFESSIONAL RELATIONSHIP ACCELERATION: FINDING STRATEGIC AND CAREER THREATS	Clients want to work with providers who understand their industry, market, company, and individual situation. Yet providers tend to define themselves as vendors by either prematurely pitching or initiating tactical questioning.	SR can initiate a strategic discussion by asking about strategic changes and challenges, and follows up on strategic problems with questions that determine CID—cause, impact, done, doing, considering, and so on—even those not related to their services. Client shares strategic issues.
PROFESSIONAL RELATIONSHIP ACCELERATION: FINDING SERVICE-RELATED PROBLEMS	Service Value is in problems providers solve not in capabilities offered. To find value in the mind of the client, providers should be proficient in uncovering motivation and resistance to service-related problems.	SR is able to smoothly redirect conversations to service-related problems using give-and-take questions, follow up with CID questions, and then gain agreement to explore solutions. Client agrees to explore solutions.

(Continued)

PROPERTY/PROJECT DIFFERENCE: FINDING UNIQUE PROPERTY/ PROJECT/MARKET CHARACTERISTICS	Clients prefer to work with providers who understand their unique property/ project/market. Yet some SR tend to rely on comparable research and not explore unique property/project/market characteristics	SR asks questions to uncover unique property/project/market characteristics and project fit in overall strategy. Client shares critical information not included in RFP.
PREFERENCE DIFFERENCE: FINDING UNIQUE CLIENT PREFERENCES FROM PREVIOUS EXPERIENCE, CURRENT CONCERNS, CLIENT VISIONS, AND COMPETITION	Client decision makers are heavily influenced by their previous experience, current concerns, visions, and competitive alternatives. Yet some SR fail to explore and align to unique client preferences and instead tend to fit clients to their services.	SR asks questions about client's previous experience, current concerns, visions, and competitive alternatives to uncover unique preferences and criteria. Client willing to share preferences that create competitive advantage.
PROCESS DIFFERENCE: ACCESSING DECISION MAKERS AND INFLUENCERS TO DETERMINE AND INFLUENCE DECISION PROCESS.	If SR are not dealing directly with decision makers, they are at greater risk of losing or competing on price because they are not able to achieve Third-Level differentiation.	SR is able to identify and access key decision makers and influencers and build preference with each. SR is able to present persuasive argument to gain access. Client shares decision process and allows access.
ALIGNING TO VALUE	SR may offer solutions either prematurely or offer solutions out of alignment with client motivation or decision stage. That slows or stalls the decision and creates unproductive work.	SR understands and aligns to five decision stages. SR effectively reads client motivation and resistance and makes recommendations and proposals that are better aligned to each client.

(Continued)

TEACHING POINT	PERFORMANCE ISSUE	PERFORMANCE OBJECTIVE
MOMENTUM RECOMMENDATIONS	SR may miss opportunities to advance a decision or create unnecessary work because they don't recognize decision stages or offer recommendations that advance decisions and build commitment.	At the end of client calls, SR makes specific recommendations aligned to client motivation or decision stage that advance the decision and that require clients to commit to an appropriate next step. Client agrees to next step and takes action.
CLIENT-CENTRIC PRESENTATIONS	Clients perceive little differences in the capabilities of their top service provider choices. Yet SR tend to focus their offer on their vendor differentiators, instead of client differentiators to differentiate themselves from competitors.	In presentations and proposals SR presents unique client problems, objectives, situation, and preferences first, then gains agreement before offering aligned solutions and differentiation. Client agrees with summary of client differentiators.
ALIGNED DIFFERENTIATION	Providers tend to use generic, undifferentiated (Airbag) language, which makes it difficult for clients to choose them over competitors.	SR presents relevant and aligned difference, preference, and proof based upon client stated execution issues so that clients choose them at the same or better price. Proof includes relevant story, benchmark results, and specific client testimonial. Client chooses SR away from price.

If the sales representative is not achieving the performance objectives above, you can use the Deliberate Practice activities at the end of each chapter to coach and reinforce the skills. You can formalize continuous improvement by incorporating the Deliberate Practice into your regular meetings and day-to-day interactions with your sales people. You can also use the client profile.

At the end of my Third-Level workshops, I give the client profile with questions (Figure 9.3 and Appendix 4) to participants; this tool can be used as a training summary, diagnostic, preparation, and coaching tool as well as a foundation for a client-centric presentation or recommendation. It is both the map and the navigation for Third-Level Selling. Here are a few suggestions on how to use the client profile as a coaching tool.

CALL PREPARATION AND MOMENTUM RECOMMENDATIONS

Before your next joint call, ask the sales representative to fill out a client profile. How rich is the information in each segment? Does the information come from the client or are they just assumptions? Where is information lacking? Ask the sales rep what questions they will ask to fill out missing client differentiation in the upcoming call?

Ask the sales rep what the possible outcomes of the call will be. Have him/her identify and practice best-case and worst-case momentum recommendations. What will they ask the client to do at the end of the call?

Ideally the client will do most of the talking during the meeting. Save the last few minutes for your recommendations. If the allotted time for your meeting is one hour, let the client talk and save the last 10 minutes for your recommendations.

If possible, role-play the conversation and recommendations in advance. Even though role-playing feels awkward and remedial, particularly for veteran providers, it is the best way to build competence and mastery. Use it. It's like taking practice shots on the driving range after a golf lesson. You will want to master new skills before applying them in a stressful situation.

CALL REVIEW AND DIAGNOSTICS

After the client meeting ask the sales rep to self-diagnose the call first. This will help them learn to self-coach going forward. What went well? What could be improved? Now bring out the client profile. Ask the rep to evaluate if he/she was able to get any or all of the critical information.

- Personal Relationship: Is the rep acquiring and deepening personal common ground (amazing story), or do they just have a few personal facts about the client?
- Professional Relationship: Do they have a deep understanding about the client's key strategic issues, or are they assuming general market conditions?
- Project/Property Difference: Have they learned more about the project/property than what is listed in the RFP or than what the competition knows?
- Preference Difference: Have they uncovered critical and unique client preferences? Do they know about previous projects, who did it, what worked, what did not, what concerns the client has about this project, what the client's vision for the best approach or outcome is, who they are competing with, and what the client's perceptions of strengths and weaknesses are?

- Decision Process: Can they tell you exactly when the decision will be made, who will make it, and how? Did they get access to the real decision maker?
- Momentum Recommendation: Was their momentum recommendation appropriate? Was it aligned with the decision stage? Did it advance the decision? And, most importantly, was the client asked to and did the client agree to take an action that demonstrated commitment?

If so, great; that rep is working at the Third Level. Invite them to mentor others. That will groom them for manager roles to come. If not, where are the gaps? This is not the time to play "gotcha" to show how much you know. It's a learning opportunity for both of you. Missing areas will guide you to the specific questions to practice to build skills. Once again, if your reps are consistently getting good client information, I don't care if they use the questions that I suggest or the ones that seem to be working for them. It's the outcome we are looking for.

COACHING

If they are consistently missing one or more of the five areas in the client profile, then those are the areas to focus your coaching efforts. Refer back to the questions I suggest if the rep has not developed some of his/her own.

Once again, role-playing is the best way to build communication skills, but it is usually resisted. By actually executing the behavior, reps frequently discover the difference between knowing what should be done and being able to do it. So don't let them off the hook by describing what they would do. Have them do it. Better to try it and make mistakes with you than to make mistakes in front of the client.

PRESENTATIONS AND RECOMMENDATIONS

The objective of Third-Level Selling is to get people focused on what is unique about the client because it yields more room to differentiate and it builds a sense of partnership. Presentations and recommendations should reflect that client-centric bent and focus on the client, not on capabilities. That means taking all of that great client differentiation information on the client profile and showing clients that you "feel their pain" by feeding back client problems, concerns, objectives, situation, and constraints and then verifying them before presenting your difference, preference, and proof.

Your continuous coaching and reinforcement is the best way to migrate your team from a self-defeating vendor-centric culture to an elite client-centric culture. It is also the best way for you to achieve your own career goals.

Chapter 14

Final Thoughts

The objective of this book is to help you sell less, win more, and have more fun. My premise is that the more you are aligned with prospective clients, the more likely you are to win their business. This is more important than ever in these hyper-competitive times.

The more you know about how and why the real estate service buyer makes the decision to choose a particular service provider, the more you can align your message and service solution to fit the client's need, situation, and decision-making process.

I would estimate that 80 percent of real estate providers are stuck at the vendor level. They believe that their value is in their capabilities, so they spend their time making cold calls and pitching. They do most of the talking in client meetings because they assume that the more the client knows about them, the more likely the client is to choose them. In essence they are shooting the shotgun in the air and hoping a duck flies over. Vendors can be successful, but they have to work much harder to win. Their win rate tends to be low because they cannot communicate how they are different or better.

About 15 percent of service providers compete at the preferred provider level. They engage clients tactically, find client needs for their services, and are able to communicate that their capabilities and approach are better. They usually accomplish this by specializing enough to be the highest-ranking provider in a niche. That makes it easier for clients to choose them. They do enough

The Third Level

1. Vendors –
Pitch Capabilities

2. Preferred Provider –
Position versus Competition

3. Strategic Partners –
Differentiate on the Client

Figure 14.1 Partners Win More, Retain More, Advance Further, and Enjoy It More.

business to tell good stories about clients in similar situations and have testimonials from well-known clients. But they tend to view clients as similar and offer the same tried and true solutions that help them establish and maintain their rank. Their clients are satisfied because preferred providers can take care of it as well as anyone.

The top 5 percent of service providers are viewed not just as competent solution providers, but also as partners. Clients know, like, and trust them. They feel that their partners have a deep understanding of them personally and professionally. Third-Level providers know the property, preferences, and process better so they can make decisions and implement solutions that not only take care of it, but also take care of the client. Clients feel that their partners will assume their burden and get the best possible outcome whatever it takes. That frees the client to work on other critical areas of their business.

Clients of partners tend to be highly satisfied. They don't look for alternative providers. They don't even talk to competitors.

They are less price sensitive and more forgiving. They not only give their partners follow-on business without competition, they actively sell for their partners in the marketplace. They become the partner's surrogate sales force. So partners rarely have to sell.

I am convinced that mastering the art of Third-Level Selling makes it faster and easier to win. Migrating from pitch to position by understating and articulating difference, preference, and proof will allow you to survive the screening phase. By demonstrating your understanding of the client—personally, professionally, their project, preferences, and decision process—and your commitment to the project you will build emotional preference to win the business. Finally, by using Third-Level principles with all client stakeholders across an organization, you will win the relationship.

I don't believe you can become proficient in Third-Level Selling by spending a couple of hours reading this book any more than I believe you can become a top chef by reading *The Joy of Cooking*. Service selling at the executive level is an extremely complex interaction with unlimited variations. A book that would try to capture it all would collapse under its own weight.

Mastery comes with time, diligence, review, and deliberate practice. But you need help now, so let me give you a few quick tips that will work for you immediately.

GET WITH CLIENTS

I had lunch the other day with a tenant rep leasing broker who had been in the business for 25 years but was still grinding away trying to find new clients. He had asked for my help. When we met, he handed me a packet of all the new collateral materials, letters, and research pieces he planned to send to potential clients. He spent weeks working on it.

He felt that if he got enough good information in the marketplace more people would ask for help. I hated to pop his balloon after so much work, but marketing doesn't sell services. Increased market awareness will get you invited to compete, but it does not win the business.

I learned that with my first book. I wrote it to avoid cold-calling. My thinking was that when people read my book they would invite me in because of my experience and capabilities. As it turned out only about 5 percent of my business comes from readers who I don't already know. Ninety-five percent of my work comes from people I know or from the people whom they know and have referred me.

I told my friend that he should stop writing and get in front of potential clients. Use your existing clients as a referral platform, and use your research as a quid pro quo for the meeting. Even if you don't do it well, there is no substitute for this type of direct interaction. You can't differentiate on clients from a distance. You have to go face-to-face.

ENLIGHTENED SELF-INTEREST

I have given you the navigation tools to migrate from vendor to preferred provider to partner. I did that by offering theories and deliberate practice. But that is not enough. Just doing the right things without the right attitude will make you seem manipulative. To be truly client-centric your attitude must lead your behavior. Being a partner is more about attitude than it is technique.

At its core, providing a service means helping. You became a service professional because you wanted to use your expertise to help clients achieve their objectives. Although you are well paid, client appreciation is the intrinsic compensation that brings the most career satisfaction.

You get what you want only if the client gets what he or she wants, so forget everything that you have read here while you are with the prospect. Your only concern is to help the prospect optimally align to his or her market. Forget your solutions, your capabilities, and even the questions that this book suggests to ask next. It's all about the prospective client. Anything that distracts you from focusing on and listening to the prospect undermines trust. If you are thinking about what Potter told you to do next, you are not engaged.

There will be plenty of time to review and plan when you are not face to face with the prospect. Good luck.

Appendix 1

BCCI Value Proposition

Here is an example that demonstrates how changing the focus of your market offer from a capabilities-based message to a problem/objective message can add value and accelerate your message. A few years ago I worked with BCCI, a commercial contractor located in the Bay Area. They felt that their message was too generic. So we mapped contractor services from the client prospective and identified major concerns that most clients faced when taking on a tenant improvement project.

We saw that clients were concerned that the contractor may not fully grasp their and their designer's vision for the property. If the contractor failed to grasp or did not reconcile visions with a budget, the client's expectations would not be met and the project would fail.

Clients were also concerned about surprises that cause missed budgets and blown schedules that would make them look bad to their constituents. Finally, clients were concerned that the finished product be truly finished without long punch lists or poor quality that would cause a messy transition to the new space.

BCCI developed a problem-based message that they refer to as the Four Pillars of Success. With their permission I have included their offer here. Notice how BCCI addresses their message to client execution concerns and objectives instead of just listing capabilities.

BCCI's Four Pillars of Success:

1. Vision Collaboration
2. Pinpoint Planning
3. Seamless Execution
4. Flawless Delivery

1. Vision Collaboration

Our clients want to be confident that they are creating the best possible space solution for their people. They want us to understand, challenge, test, and expand their vision. They want us to share and be committed to its realization within their budget and time constraints. Our clients are looking for partners. We collaborate with them to create and envision their best possible space solution. We explore form, function, image, budget, timing, and special circumstances.

It is unusual for a construction firm to be so involved in the planning stages of a project. At BCCI, we believe that the more we understand, share and own our client's vision, the better we can plan for and deliver it. If we can anticipate and eliminate waste, we can use that time and money to give our clients more.

2. Predictability from Pinpoint Planning

Our clients want to feel comfortable and confident that we can and will deliver their vision. They want a clear and accurate plan to assure that they reach their vision smoothly and painlessly, on time and on budget. They need to be able to rely on us to predict what is going to happen, when, and for how much in order to plan their own resource allocations and help their staff/internal clients plan their transition into the new or renovated space.

Collaboration during preconstruction creates a clear and shared vision of the outcome; pinpoint preconstruction planning creates a clear and shared vision of the building process. It anticipates and eliminates controllable delays, surprises, and cost overruns; the better the plan the smoother the process. It is in everyone's interest to eliminate surprises. This is why BCCI creates the most comprehensive budget, logistics, and schedule plan available.

3. Commitment to Seamless Execution

Being on time and on budget is not enough. Our clients want a frictionless and transparent process that eliminates surprises. They want us to have anticipated and planned away the controllable, and they want us to handle the uncontrollable on our own. They want us to be responsive and flexible to changes. Our clients want us to "own" the project.

The beauty is what is not seen. Ninety percent of delays and cost overruns are caused by predictable and controllable events. Shared vision and pinpoint planning eliminate wasted time and money. BCCI delivers superior results because controllable delays and disruptions that blow up budgets and schedules just don't happen on our projects. The client doesn't hear about material delays, permit hang-ups, labor mismanagement, or uncoordinated workflow. Uncontrollable surprises are contained.

4. Trust in a Flawless Delivery

The final stages of the project create a lasting impression. Our clients want their people to transition into their new space without delay or disruption. They want a clean, complete, and fully functional environment where their people feel good and work well.

They want us to find and fix flaws, make sure materials, furniture, fixtures, and systems are in place and fully operational. In fact, they don't want a punch-list to be necessary at all. They want a delivery without flaws.

BCCI not only talks the talk, they also worked hard to align their processes and people to match their value proposition. As a result, both their win rate and client retention is among the highest in the industry.

Appendix 2

Company Message Acceleration Example

Here's an example of message acceleration in action at the company level. I worked with a real estate brokerage firm whose only offices were in New York City. This company was having difficulty winning competitive business against large national concerns. When asked to describe their services, they said they were committed to good service, had good market knowledge, offered full service expertise, had two NYC offices and had seasoned professionals in their employ. Initially, their message looked like this:

Message Acceleration Chart

UNIQUE SERVICE (BRANDED)	DIFFERENCE? (HOW IS IT DIFFERENT?)	PREFERENCE? ("SO WHAT?" WHY IS IT IMPORTANT TO THIS CLIENT?)	PROOF (WHAT EVIDENCE DO YOU HAVE TO PROVE IT?)
Committed to good service Good market knowledge Full service expertise NYC offices			

These are all excellent attributes but hardly unique. These characteristics are classic airbags—important but undistinguished. What brokerage company doesn't say they work hard, offer good service, and have experience?

All the same, this firm's existing clients loved them, so I asked the real estate company executives what they had done for their existing clients that set them apart from the national companies and used that to build their value proposition.

How Are You Different? (Difference)

"Most of the nationals pitch the business with the experienced brokers, but the work is actually done by junior people who work on transactions all over the Northeast. In our case, all aspects of the transaction are handled by professionals with at least 20 years of experience in New York City. Our clients never have to deal with rookies."

So What? Why Is That Important to the Client? (Preference)

"Most New York properties are sold or leased to other New Yorkers. We know the market, and we know how to execute the deal. We know who is active, what they are looking for, and what they can pay. We have all done hundreds of deals, so we can get it done with fewer mistakes and fewer surprises."

So What? (Preference) What Do Fewer Mistakes and Surprises Mean to the Client? (Author's hint: keep probing preference value until you reach the financial impact or risk impact.)

"Slow execution exposes sellers to market risk and ties up their funds. Our clients receive faster and smoother execution from us, which translates into less market risk and more liquidity."

Can You Give Evidence That Your Preference Value Yields Better Results? (Proof)

The real estate firm was able to demonstrate consistently faster asset sales averaging between 90 days and 120 days. They offered a story about matching up a buyer and seller on one transaction where neither the buyer nor seller wanted their positions to be public. This firm was able to bring them together because of their deep knowledge of the local market. The firm also provided evidence in the form of specific testimonials from existing clients that favorably compared their performance to national firms. One institutional investor said, "When it comes to New York dispositions, I will only use them." They branded their execution capabilities "No Rookies Execution" to emphasize their unique transaction experience. Now take a look at their value chart.

Message Acceleration Chart

UNIQUE SERVICE	DIFFERENCE	PREFERENCE	PROOF
"No Rookies Execution" Team	Buyer and seller will only deal with someone with at least 20 years of NYC experience	Faster execution Fewer mistakes Less market risk More liquidity	Comparative stories and testimonials 90- to 120-day dispositions Resumes "In New York I only work with them."

With a newly found awareness of and ability to articulate their accelerated message, this company was able to turn weakness into strength.

"Our *No Rookies Execution* means that you and potential investors will only deal with a professional who has had at least 20 years of experience in New York City. That means higher-quality representation, faster execution, fewer mistakes, and more liquidity. That also means no more handholding junior staff through the process. On average, our dispositions close within 90 to 120 days of initial marketing. Here are the résumés of our *No Rookies Team*. We recently completed a disposition for an institutional client for a class A office building in Midtown. We knew a motivated buyer ready to move immediately and had the deal done in 90 days. That client says that when he has dispositions in New York City, 'I will only work with them.'"

The *No Rookies* brand successfully positioned their reliable execution and made the nationals seem riskier. National firms may be broader, but now this local firm could prove they were deeper and more experienced in this market.

Client Profile

Third Level™ Client Profile

1. **Personal: Common Ground?**
   Personal Client Info: (Time in position, previous, family, schooling, interests, common ground, etc.)

   >

2. **Professional: Strategic and Deal-Related Problems?**
   Client Perception of Key Changes:

   >

   Client Strategic Problems that could threaten career or company:

   >

   Key real estate problem or objective you could support: How:

   >

3. **Project/Property Difference?**
   Unique Project/Property Characteristics that impact risk, price, timing, execution:

   >

4. **Preferences Difference?**
   Previous Experience, Concerns, Client's Visions, Competition:

   >

5. **Client Decision Process?** (Timing People, Decision Process?)

   >

   Your Proof Statement For This Client?: Difference, Preference, Proof?

   >

   Decision Stage and Momentum Recommendation:

   >

Appendix 4

Client Profile with Questions

1. **Personal: Common Ground?**
   Personal Client Info: (Time in position, previous, family, schooling, interests, common ground, etc.)

   > ☐ How long in this position?
   > ☐ What did you do before?
   > ☐ Did you grow up and do your schooling here?
   > ☐ Do you live in the area?

2. **Professional: Strategic and Deal Related Problems?**
   Client Perception of Key Industry, Market, Company, or Internal Changes:

   > What changes are you seeing in ......
   > ☐ Industry, market, company, property usage, investment strategy, role?
   > ☐ Tenant retention?
   > ☐ Encroachment by competitors?
   > ☐ Rental rates? Etc.

   Key Client Strategic Problems that could threaten career or company:

   > When the client shares any problem above, explore it for CID:
   > ☐ Cause?
   > ☐ Impact?
   > ☐ Done, Doing, Considering

   Key real estate problem or objective you could support: How:

   > ☐ What caused you to pursue this project?
   >   o **CID**—Cause? Impact? What else considered?
   > ☐ Why now?
   > ☐ What are your objectives? What are your constraints?

3. **Project/Property Difference?** (Unique Project/Property Characteristics that impact risk, price, timing, execution):

   > ☐ What caused you to pursue this project?
   >   o **CID**—Cause? Impact? What else considered?
   > ☐ Why now?
   > ☐ How does this fit into your overall strategy?
   > ☐ What is unique or unusual about this property?

Third Level™ Client Profile (With Questions)

4. Preferences Difference? (Previous Experience, Concerns, Client's Visions, Competition):

- ☐ Tell me about previous projects?
- ☐ Who did it? What went well? What didn't?
- ☐ What caused that? How did that impact you?
- ☐ What are your concerns about. . .risk, effort, timing?
- ☐ What do you think is the best way to approach this?
- ☐ What are looking you for? Criteria
- ☐ Who else is invited?
- ☐ How would you compare us now?
- ☐ What alternative approaches look attractive? Why?

5. Client Decision Process? (Timing, People, Decision Process?)

- ☐ Who else will be involved in this decision? What role will they play? What are their criteria? Can we meet with them?
- ☐ When does this need to be completed? Why?
- ☐ How will the decision be made?

Your Proof Statement For This Client?: Difference, Preference, Proof?

What can you provably do better than your best competitor to achieve this client's execution objective? Why can you get them a better outcome than anyone else? What is your proof? (Story, benchmark and testimonial)

Decision Stage and Momentum Recommendation:

What stage? 1. Awareness 2. Assessment 3. Search 4. Evaluation 5. Provider
Recommendation that 1. Fits stage 2. Advances decision 3. Client action
What is best possible outcome? What will you ask the client to do?
What is the least expected outcome? What will you ask the client to do?

About the Author

Robert A. Potter is the managing principal of R. A. Potter Advisors, LLC, a commercial real estate strategic marketing and sale strategy consulting firm that shows companies and providers how to accelerate their message and relationships to win and retain clients. His clients include some of the best-known real estate service firms.

He is the author of *Winning in the Invisible Market: A Guide to Selling Professional Services in Turbulent Times*. Bob spent 25 years in sales and business development for IBM, McGraw-Hill, Dean Witter, and MBIA. He has opened new markets in the United States, Mexico, Australia, and Asia. Several years ago he co-founded and then sold REALBID (a successful commercial real estate technology company), to COMPS, and then to Costar Group, and started R. A. Potter Advisors to help other service providers win and retain clients.

He received his B.A. degree from Santa Clara University and his M.B.A from UC Berkeley. He lives with his wife and sons in San Anselmo, CA.

Bob Potter has written articles for dozens of magazines, and he is a frequent speaker at national meetings and industry conferences. If you would like more information, please go to www.rapotter.com or contact Bob at bpotter@rapotter.com.

Index

10-year rule, 17

A

Acceleration:
  corporate message example,
    191–194
  personal relationships, 67–78
  professional relationships, 62,
    63, 79–89
Access, gaining, 157–159
Accountability, performance
    metrics and, 172
Advocates, client, 143, 150–151
Agreement, verifying and
    gaining, 125–126
  to search for solutions, 87–89
Airbags, 2–4, 11–13
America's Brokerage, 137
Anderson, Jerry, 40
Anecdote, positioning message
    and, 45–47
Approach:
  differentiation, 25
  preferred providers and,
    54
Asset-backed financing, 156
Assumption:
  client-centric, 14–16
  vendor-centric, 12–13

B

Bain & Company, 144
BCCI, 49–50
  value proposition, 187–190
Benchmark, 45

C

Calls:
  preparation, 177–178
  resistance to cold, 70
  review, 178–179
Capabilities:
  differentiation, 25
  preferred providers and, 54
  vendor-pitched, 8
Capital, inefficient use of,
    156
Cash flows, how to value, 12
Cause. *See* CID, looking for
Chambers, George, 94–95
CID:
  client preferences and, 110
  decision-making process and,
    114
  invisible market, 160–161
  looking for, 84–85
Citi Realty Services, 95
  negotiations and, 136–137
Coaching, 179–180

Cold calling. *See* Calls,
    resistance to cold
Coldwell Banker Commercial,
    40
Colliers International, 28
  project/property difference
    and, 93–95
  selection phase and, 33
Colton, Jeff, 76–77
Commitment, invisible market
    and, 163–165
Communication:
  airbag messages and, 3
  non-verbal, 32
Competition:
  changes with, 83
  client preferences and,
    107–110
  as motivation, 172
  vs. position, 39–43
  preferred provider positioned
    against, 8–9, 13–14
Cost. *See* Pricing
Customer Satisfaction Survey
    (CSS), 149
Cuthbert, Peter, 30–31, 94

D
Decision funnel:
  client satisfaction and,
    146–147
  provider, 23
Decision making, 21–24
  deliberate practice, 35–36
  differentiation and, 24–28, 60,
    61, 63

finding and aligning the
    process, 113–118
hierarchy, 24, 54
invisible market and, 161–162
  five stages of service
    decision, 162–163
  momentum
    recommendations,
    163–166
  pricing and negotiating,
    137–140
  provider decision funnel,
    23
  SLIRE example, 28–33
Delivery, flawless, 188, 189–190
Demand, changes in, 83
Diagnostics, third-level, 64–65
Differentiation, 5–11, 24, 61
  aligned, observable
    performance objectives
    and, 176
  approach, 25
  capabilities, 25, 54
  decision-making, 24–25, 60,
    61, 63
  offers, 2–4
  personal relationships, 24, 60,
    61, 63
  preferences, 60, 61, 63
    observable performance
      objectives, 175
  professional relationships, 24,
    60, 61, 63
  project/property, 25, 60, 61, 63,
    91–99
  vendor, 5–11, 25

Disruption:
  best outcomes and, 52–53
  preferences and, 101
Domination, market. *See* Value
  zone, specialization of
DPR Construction, 149

E
Effort, preferences and, 101
Ericsson, Anders, 17
Execution:
  preferences as client
    differentiators, 25
  seamless, 188, 189
Experience:
  defining, 49–50
  as a driver of preferences,
    102–103
  preferred providers and, 54
  as a vendor differentiator, 25
  See also Position; Rank

F
Familiarity. *See* Personal
  relationships
Feedback, client-centric
  proposals and
  presentations, 125
Flexibility, 38
Fortune 1000 companies, 97
Four Pillars of Success, 187–190

G
GAAP, 137
Generalist trap, 38–39
Gensler, 75

client-centric proposals and
  presentations, 121–122
Golf Digest, 18
Grubb & Ellis, 80, 81

H
Hake, Rich, 134
Hess, Bob, 97–98

I
Impact. *See* CID, looking for
Interest rates, changes to,
  83
Invisible market, 153–155
  deliberate practice, 166–167
  service decision, finding and
    aligning, 161–166
  unqualified clients and,
    155–161

J
Johanson, Lori:
  negotiations and, 136–137
  project/property difference
    and, 95–96

K
Kipling Capital, 134

L
Legal issues, 83
Likeability, teaching, 75
Loyalty, client satisfaction and,
  143–146
Loyalty Rules, 144
Ludeman, Chris, 137–138

M

Meetings, as transactions,
158–159
Meissner, Tim, 135–136
Meissner Jacquet Investment
Management Services,
135–136
Mobley, Shawn, 80, 81
Momentum:
call preparation and, 177–178
invisible market and, 163–165
observable performance
objectives and, 176
Motivation, selling skills and,
171–172

N

Negotiation, 134
personal relationships and,
134–135
professional relationships and,
135–136

O

Objectives:
isolating, 125–127
negotiating strategic, 136
observable performance,
173–176
Observable performance
objectives. *See*
Objectives, observable
performance
Outcomes, defining, 50–53
Outsourcing, project/property
difference and, 93

P

Partnership, establishing a, 59–65
Performance metrics, tracking,
170–172
Personal relationships:
accelerating, 62, 63, 67–70
common ground, 70–71
deliberate practice, 78
fake sincerity, 77–78
maintaining, 75–76
observable performance
objectives and, 174
questioning, 71–75
selling time, appropriate,
76–77
differentiation and, 24, 60, 61,
63
as a driver of choice, 28
negotiation and, 134–135
Pinpoint planning, 188–189
Position:
competition and, 39–43
difference, preference, and
proof, 43–47, 56–57
See also Experience; Rank
PowerPoint, customizing, 62
Predictability, 188–189
Preferences:
differentiation, 60, 61, 63, 175
finding and aligning to client,
101–102
competition, 107–109
unhooking the, 109–110
deliberate practice, 110–112
educating concerns,
103–105

previous experience,
102–103
risk evaluation, 105–106
vision, 106–107
understanding, 60
Presentations, client-centric,
79–80, 119–124
agreement, verify and gain,
125
client profile, 123–124
deliberate practice, 128–129
isolating objectives, 125–127
observable performance
objectives and, 176
selecting the presenter,
127–128
unique feedback, 125
Pricing, 131–134, 140
avoiding as a differentiator,
53–54
preferences and, 101, 103
preferred providers and,
54
as a vendor differentiator, 25
Professional relationships:
accelerating, 62, 63
deliberate practice, 89–90
gaining agreement to
explore solutions, 87–89
observable performance
objectives and, 174
questioning and, 81–82
changes, 82–83
CID, 84–85
give and take, 86–87
research and, 80–81

differentiation and, 24, 60, 61,
63
negotiation and, 135–136
Profile, client, 195
with questions, 197–198
Project/property differentiation,
25
client differentiation and, 60,
61, 63
finding, 91–99
observable performance
objectives and, 175
Proof:
positioning, 44–47, 56–57
preferred providers and, 54
rank as, 48–49
as a vendor differentiator, 25
Property difference. *See*
Project/property
differentiation
Proposals, client-centric,
119–122
agreement, verifying and
gaining, 125
client profile, 123–124
deliberate practice, 128–129
isolating objectives, 125–127
selecting the presenter,
127–128
unique feedback, 125

Q
Questioning, 71–73
accelerating professional
relationships
strategic, 81, 82–83

Questioning (*Continued*)
    tactical, 81
    competition and, 108
    decision-making process and,
        113–114
    preferences and, 105–106,
        108
    using caution with, 74–75

R
Rank, 26–27, 48–49. *See also*
        Experience; Position
Regulations, changes in, 83
Reichheld, Fred, 144, 150
Relationships. *See* Personal
        relationships; Professional
        relationships
Religion, avoiding questions
        about, 74–75
Requests for information (RFI):
    project/property difference
        and, 93–94, 95
    search phase and, 29
Request for proposal (RFP):
    accelerating personal
        relationships and, 67–68,
        80–81
    avoiding low-level decision
        makers, 138–139
    client-centric proposals and
        presentations, 122
    decision making and, 23
    performance metrics and, 171
    preferences and, 110
    project/property difference
        and, 95

assumptions, 96–97
    screening phase and, 31
    search phase and, 29
    selection phase and, 34
Research:
    finding common ground and,
        73–74
    professional relationships and,
        79–81
Risk:
    best outcomes and, 51
    preferences and, 101
        educating about, 103–104
    rank and, 26–27

S
Satisfaction, client:
    accelerating personal
        relationships and, 69
    criteria, 146–148
        measuring, 148–149
    deliberate practice, 151–152
    loyalty and, 143–146
    referrals, 150–151
Screening service providers, 22,
        39–43
Searching service providers, 22,
        37–39
Selecting service providers,
        22–23
Self-fulfilling prophecy, 55
Selling skills, 169–170
    call review, 178–179
    coaching and, 173–177,
        179–180
    diagnostics, 178–179

recommendations, 177–178, 180

tracking performance metrics, 170–172

Sincerity, fake, 77

SLIRE, 28–33, 94

Smith Barney, 95

Solutions, gaining agreement to explore, 87–89

Speed, best outcomes and, 52

Sperry Van Ness, 40, 159

Standard Life Investments Real Estate (SLIRE) Inc.:
project/property difference and, 93–94
screening phase, 29–31
search phase, 28–29
selection phase, 31–32
picking battles, 33

Statement of qualifications (SOQ), search phase and, 29

Straight from the Gut, 171

Strategic questions. *See* Questioning

Surprises:
best outcomes and, 52–53
preferences and, 101

SWOT analysis, project/ property difference and, 94, 95

T

Tactical questions. *See* Questioning

Teaching points, 173–176

Technology, changes in, 83

Testimonials, client, 45
harvesting specific, 47–48

ThyssenKrupp, 97

Time, preferences and, 101

Trust, accelerating personal relationships and, 68

Tucker, Jim, 159

The Ultimate Question Driving Good Profits and True Growth, 144, 149–150

U

Unqualified clients, 155–161

Urgency, invisible market and, 165

V

ValleyCrest Landscape Development, 76
client satisfaction and, 144

Value:
aligning to, 175
observable performance objectives and, 173–176
proposition
BCCI, 187–190
career satisfaction and, 3
company example, 191–194
zone
in the invisible market, 156–157

Value (*Continued*)
   specialization of, 41–43,
     55–56
Variable rates, 156
Vendor differentiation. *See*
   Differentiation, vendor
Virtuous cycle, 149
Visible market, 154–155. *See also*
   Invisible market
Vision:
  collaboration, 188
  preferences and alignment of,
    106–107

W
The Wall Street Journal, 86
Welch, Jack, 171
"What It Takes To Be Great,"
   17
Winey, Dan:
  accelerating personal
    relationships, 75
  client-centric proposals and
    presentations, 121–122
Winning in the Invisible Market,
   153
Woods, Tiger, 16–17